PREFACE

Dear Reader,

This book is a must for new and used believers! It is written to help you serve the Lord and build up the body of Christ. It is to help you understand that you already have the tools that God wants you to use — you just need to learn how to use them. Spiritual growth accelerates when we begin helping others. Let me encourage you to get involved in ministry now!

After you finish reading this book you will know that God has given you talents, abilities, and opportunities for you to minister. Start praying now for Him to show you how you can best serve others in His Kingdom.

Serving Christ with you,
Dave Ray

How can you make the best use of this book?

The book can be read in one evening by skipping the questions at the end of each chapter. If, after reading the book, you want to apply it to your particular situation, then go back through and read the Personal Perspective Questions. These questions are designed to help you apply the chapter's teachings to your individual circumstances.

The Group Discussion Questions are designed for Sunday school and home Bible-study groups. (They also can be of value to the individual reader.) The Personal Perspective Questions are more subjective and the Group Discussion Questions more open-ended. The book is presented in 13 chapters to facilitate group study. The discussion questions are designed so that each individual church can bring in their particular distinctives. You simply read the weekly chapter before attending the session. Use the discussion questions for lively conversation and further study. We have purposely included more questions than you can cover in one session so leaders can select the questions most suitable for their group. As an additional help there is an index at the end of the book.

Acknowledgment: Many thanks to the more than fifty family and friends who helped make this book possible. May the blessings of God be upon you.

YOUR MINISTRY... anything you do to strengthen others!

Table of Contents

YOU HAVE A MINISTRY... God gave it to you!

CHAPTER ONE

> YOU CAN MAKE A DIFFERENCE.
> YOU CAN MAKE A SIGNIFICANT DIFFERENCE!
> YOU CAN MAKE A SIGNIFICANT DIFFERENCE FOR ETERNITY
> AND YOU CAN DO IT NOW!

INTRODUCTION

The Bible is clear - the world needs Christ and each believer has a Christ-centered ministry to the decaying world.

Ephesians 2:10 says, For we are God's masterpiece. He has created us anew in Christ Jesus, so that we can do the good things he planned for us long ago. Think of it — before you were born *Jeremiah 1:5* — God had already designed a ministry for you. (Other words for ministry are job, work, mission, or destiny, but ministry will be used throughout this book). The hope is that this practical book will motivate you to get involved in your ministry, give you some direction on how to start, and guide you through what you can do as you help work with others in the Body of Christ.

There is a lack of heroes today. Present day America has lowered its expectations of politicians, sports figures, media, the Church, individual Christians, each other, and even God. In a way, the 21st century church has copied the medieval monastic movement — during the middle ages monks withdrew from the world for religious reasons. By attempting to keep our spiritual life confined to our home and church we have become desensitized to the suffering of the world. Fifty million Americans consider themselves active Christians, yet at the same time are afraid to touch or be touched by anyone who does not look and think like them. We have pulled back from mainstream society. The void we have left has been filled by agencies that generally have little or nothing to do with God and His love. By segregating ourselves from the world we are losing the battle for influence over our nation and the next generation.

This is not what Jesus wants us to do. He said, *"When you put on a luncheon or a dinner, don't invite your friends, brothers, relatives, and rich neighbors. For they will repay you by inviting you back. Instead invite the poor, the crippled, the lame, and the blind. Then at the resurrection of the godly, God will reward you for inviting those who could not repay you." Luke 14:12-14* (**Read** *Luke 14:7-14* for the whole story.) The Bible is clear -- the world needs Christ and each believer has a Christ-centered ministry to the decaying world. However, when today's Christians discuss changing the world, after all the talk is said and done, there is a lot more said than done.

Many American Christians come from strongly confessional and/or doctrinal church backgrounds. They may be unaccustomed to ministering in ways not practiced by their fellowship or joining in ministry with those outside of their local church. Because of this, there are often missed opportunities in fulfilling the commandment to love your neighbor. This book is a plea for Christians to do ministry for the sake of the hurting and the lost. It encourages work within the local church. The ministry you choose may sometimes be outside of the scope of activities or theological framework of your church fellowship, but within the scope of God's command for us. Be assured that these activities will do no harm to those strongly confessional and/or doctrinal churches, and may bring them a new and healthy perspective.

I am a layman, not a theologian, but through life experiences and opportunities I have been challenged to get involved and have done so. This book shares some of the experiences and the insights I have gained while working in ministry. You, too, can perform your God-given ministry and you can start now. The goal is to awaken Christians to the fact that God has gifted each one for a ministry. **Even if you are a brand new believer, you have a ministry. You need to be working in your God-given ministry!**

A few years after my conversion I felt that becoming a Christian had so significantly changed my world view that it was time to write my life's purpose statement. Here is the fruit of that work:

> ### DAVE RAY'S
> ### LIFE'S PURPOSE STATEMENT
> To live for God, glorifying Him,
> and enjoying His creation
> with a life of service
> under the control of and
> empowered by the Holy Spirit.
>
> Wedding my special abilities to
> God's opportunities
> in such a way as to be
> an appropriate representative
> for Christ.

Please notice, "Wedding my special abilities to God's opportunities." This means I seek work in my strength area. I don't do something someone else can do, unless there isn't anyone else to do it. Rather, I try primarily to serve in the areas of my skills and experiences. God gave me unique planning, management, and business experience. When I am using these gifts for God, I am making the best use of my time. Whenever you can be used in your proven strength areas, it is just plain good stewardship to do so. (Maybe that's why He gave us these gifts and strengths?) While I have painted walls, moved gravel, and washed dishes — I am best used when I am helping acquire land for the church, developing a position description, suggesting a budget format or a vision statement.

Don't wait for the church leaders to come to you. Overcome the former attitude of not volunteering — you are a new creature in Christ Jesus. Take the initiative, review your strengths and meet with the church leaders. Then, together see how you can best serve the brethren utilizing these strengths. You may have some difficulty knowing your areas of strength. If that is the case, then ask yourself, "Where is my passion?" Whatever makes you want to cry or beat on the table — that's your passion. Does your heart go out to single moms, abused children, addicts, etc.? The area where your passion lies is a great place to begin your ministry. (Maybe that's why He gave you the passion!)

If time allows, be involved in your church and have an outside Christian ministry to which you devote your time. However, if the family suffers due to time demands, drop the outside ministry activity. God wants good Christian spouses and parents, and expects us to place those roles at the top of our priority lists. One way many have used to solve the dilemma of choosing between family and ministry is to actually involve the family in their ministry. A very important rule: Because everyone is called by Christ to take care of his or her family — always balance the needs of your family with the needs of the world — your family wins all ties! *1 Timothy 5:8*

God has given you skills, talents and strengths to put to use. You have a ministry!

Personal Perspective Questions

1. Do you agree you have a ministry or vision? What verse comes to mind?
2. When did God choose Jeremiah to minister for Him? How did he respond? How is his response like your response? What did God promise? *Jeremiah 1:4-6*
3. When did God plan your ministry? *Ephesians 2:10* Does God's plan for you give you confidence in beginning your ministry?
4. Look again at *Ephesians 2:10*, What does God want you to do?
5. Do you believe you can make a difference? Why or why not?
6. What abilities/strengths do you have?
7. Is there any other ministry doing what you want to do? If so, are you willing to assist them?
8. How are you using your gifts and strengths in the best way within the church?
9. Are you using your strengths or wanting ones someone else has?
10. What is your life purpose?
11. Where is your passion?
12. Does an evaluation of your current responsibilities allow time for a ministry?
13. How much time each month does your schedule allow for ministry?
14. Does your church have a class to help you define your gifts?
15. Do you have a friend who could help you define your gifts or strengths?

Group Discussion Questions

1. How can you help others determine what abilities/strengths they have?
2. How can you encourage others to use these strengths?
3. Should *Christians* do good works outside their strengths?
4. What should come first: work in the church or outside? Why? *Galatians 6:10*
5. When is it okay to work in the church and the parachurch? When isn't it?
6. What should come first: family or outside ministry? *1 Timothy 5:8* Why?
7. How do you balance family needs and ministry?
8. What happens when you ignore your family? *(See 1 Samuel 2:22-25 and 3:13)*
9. How are you guilty of talking more and doing less?
10. Why do some people spend more time talking and less doing? What might be the motivation for more talking than doing?
11. In what ways are we guilty of copying the medieval monastic movement?
12. Why do some hide inside the church walls? Why do some keep silent? Why do some not try to make more of a difference outside the church?
13. To whom shall you minister? *Luke 14:7-14, Galatians 6:10*
14. When should you begin your ministry and what do you need to know before starting? (More on this in chapter 2)
15. "Because I'm not a leader I can't do a ministry." What's wrong with this reasoning?
16. Should all *Christians* be involved in at least one ministry? Why or why not?

YOU CAN MAKE A SIGNIFICANT DIFFERENCE FOR ETERNITY... YOU CAN DO IT NOW!

CHAPTER TWO

THE GOOD SAMARITAN TODAY

Put yourself in the shoes of a nonbeliever watching this incident unfold.

THE CAST

- A hurting Christian plays the parable's wounded Jew.
- A Christian preacher plays the parable's Jewish priest.
- The head of the church board plays the parable's Levite.
- An agnostic neighbor plays the parable's Samaritan.
- And introducing two new characters:
- The congregation is played by the congregation.
- You play the role of a non-believing observer.

The parable about the Good Samaritan in *Luke 10:27-37* is worth considering. You have heard many sermons about this story, and each has had a different "spin". Here's one that places the parable's characters and the story in the present day.

The story goes like this:

A Christian is sitting quietly in the pew, obviously troubled. She is lonely and confused, hurting from past abuse, and unable to overcome her dependence on alcohol. The preacher knows of her difficulty, but today he does not have the time to give her the help she needs. He is burdened with another problem to solve — word has just come that an elderly church member has taken a turn for the worse and the family has requested the pastor come to the hospital. He makes a mental note to schedule a home visit sometime in the near future; but today he just doesn't have enough time. He says a silent prayer for her, and wonders how he ever got so busy! The head of the church board is sitting in the pew three rows back. He also knows of her distress. He thinks about talking to her to see if he can help — but then he remembers — he has to drive the teens' group to the airport immediately after the service. He just can't be late or they will miss their plane for a ministry trip to Mexico. He makes a mental note to speak to the woman at the Wednesday night service if she still seems upset. At the end of the service he and his wife rush out.

The woman gets up from her pew and leaves the church. Nobody in the congregation notices her distress, and she walks out unnoticed. It is after she gets home from the Sunday service that day that a ray of hope enters her life. An agnostic neighbor of hers stops by and:

- Brings over some banana-nut bread she made.
- Doesn't hurry off but stays and listens with understanding, hugging the hurting Christian when the tears come. (Listening is always better than sharing — it's called the ministry of presence.)
- Commits to taking her to a support group she attends weekly.
- Follows through with her commitment of support.
- Buys some books to help her hurting neighbor work through her brokenness, and gives her hope. (She takes them to her the next day.)
- And finally, the agnostic says, "I'm here for you. Call me anytime you want. If you need anything more, you only need to ask."

There are two new characters in the story — the congregation and one played by you. Put yourself in the shoes of a nonbeliever watching this incident unfold. Remember, as an observer, you can only see what was happening and not what was going through the people's minds. Who would you think were the good guys? Who would you think cared? Who would you want to help you? Which would you want for a neighbor? Who acted most Christ-like? As you know, the Bible commands us to love others. *John 15:17*

To use the Good Samaritan characters from above, this book has been written to the "Congregation"!

When Jesus was asked, *"Of all the commandments, which is the most important?"* Jesus replied, *"The most important commandment is this: 'Hear, O Israel! The Lord our God is the one and only Lord. And you must love the Lord your God with all your heart, all your soul, all your mind, and all your strength.' The second is equally important: 'Love your neighbor as yourself. No other commandment is greater than these."* Mark 12: 28-31

Think about what "equally important" means? Also what does "no other commandment greater than these" mean? *"Love your neighbor as yourself"* also shows up many times in scripture. *Luke 10:27, Romans 13:9-10, Galatians 5:14, James 2:8, John 15:12,17* How can Christians help their neighbors? Our leaders are very busy trying to help but the job is just too big. What is our reasonable service as believers?

Jesus said the world would know we are Christians by our love. *John 13:34 -35* How will the world see our love when we are not acting on it? Many of us are just walking right past our hurting brothers and sisters. We are ignoring some very clear responsibilities that God has given His Church. Yet, we cannot plead ignorance, inability, or lack of opportunity. The commands to love the least, the lost and our neighbor are in the Bible for all to see. The reason Jesus told the parable of the Good Samaritan was to clarify who our neighbors are, and show how we are to love them. This love is simply doing the right thing in a given circumstance. This is the "Golden Rule" Jesus talks about in *Matthew 7:12, Do for others what you would like them to do for you. This is a summary of all that is taught in the law and the prophets.* Also keep in mind that we have been given abilities and skills with which to demonstrate this love. Furthermore, we are all given opportunities almost daily to minister to others along the way.

Think back to the parable one more time. The pastor and head of the church board had to do other things for the church —what about the

PONDER THE FOLLOWING:

Consider how we take care of the widows and orphans. How about the elderly, poor, or sick? What about criminals and their families? There is also the education of our children to think about— whose responsibility is that? *Deuteronomy 6:6-7* says that it is a parent's responsibility to either teach or make sure to monitor what is taught to his children. Today we are letting the Good Samaritan government and pagan organizations educate our children, feed the poor, and help the widows and orphans. In other words, they are doing the work Christ entrusted to you and me.

rest of the congregation? Haven't you walked by many that were suffering? What might you hear when you are called to give an account? *2 Corinthians 5:10*

The time has come for you to get out into the world and show to others the life-changing love and forgiveness that God's grace has given you. It is clear that we must begin by loving fellow Christians. *Galatians 6:10* This is your first witness: outsiders need to see your love for others. Only then will they know you are a Christian by your love. *John 13:35* Indeed, what kind of witness will you have if you're telling the world about Jesus and neglecting your hurting brothers and sisters? Will the world want to be part of God's family if you don't take care of other believers? Once Christians are known for their love, then you can freely take the message of hope into the world — reaching across social barriers to the people on the "other side." You were saved to do the good work of helping to care for others. These are called "caregiving" ministries. They are not only for your leaders but they are for you, too!

What is this book about? The Ten Commandments contain four commandments governing our relationship with God and six that govern our relationship with other people. These commandments are summarized by Jesus in *Matthew 22:37-40, "You must love the Lord your God with all your heart, all your soul, and all your mind. This is the first and greatest commandment. The second is equally important: 'Love your neighbor as yourself.' All the other commandments and all the demands of the prophets are based on these two commandments."* The Ten Commandments give a couple ways of showing love to your neighbor by <u>not doing something</u> to them—don't murder, steal, covet, etc.. The <u>doing something</u> aspects include the message of this book—to do good works of help, mercy, and kindness to your neighbor in the name of Jesus Christ. The man-directed commandments are summed up in "The Golden Rule," *Matthew 7:12 "Do for others what you would like them to do for you. This is the summary of all that is taught in the law and the prophets."*

Personal Perspective Questions
1. Why did Jesus tell the parable of the Good Samaritan? How does it apply to you?
2. What do nonbelievers see as they watch you?
3. In *Mark 12:28-31* who are you to "love" and how much are you to love them?
4. Do you agree "you are all given opportunities daily to minister...?" Are you responding to your opportunities? If not, why not?
5. The Good Samaritan is a minister of mercy. Can you list five situations that occur in your community where an act of mercy would be appropriate? Which of these would you be willing to do today?
6. Do you expect your church leaders to be the ones that do all the ministry of mercy in your church? What about you?

Group Discussion Questions
1. What do nonbelievers see as they watch your church? In what ways do they see you acting out *Romans 13:9-10?*
2. What debt does the Bible say that you can never repay? *Romans 13:8*
3. How can you encourage others to minister? *Hebrews 10:24*
4. Why are we to love one another? *John 13:34-35*
5. If the church body were following the verses in questions 1 through 4 above, what difference would you see?
6. *Galatians 6:10* teaches us to do good to two groups: who are these two groups?
7. Are you as a group helping or ignoring others? What can you do to change?
8. Are you willing to let others do the work God planned for you?
9. Mostly the needs are too great for the few leaders in the local church. How much should you expect from them? The congregation? What shouldn't you expect?
10. How can you let leadership know that you want to do more works of ministry, especially for others in your church?

YOU CAN MAKE A SIGNIFICANT DIFFERENCE FOR ETERNITY...
YOU CAN DO IT NOW!

CHAPTER THREE

STIRRING THE GIANT

The key to having fruit that remains is getting new believers involved and doing something right away.

I became a born-again believer at age 42. By that time, I had successfully run four businesses and company presidents were seeking my counsel. Even so, during an informal discussion with some men in my church, one man said that he just couldn't wait until the church got some mature leaders to help them in their planning and other management issues. I was stunned and hurt that this man did not even consider my proven abilities as a manager and strategic planner. To these men, my experience was of no value because I was not a spiritual heavyweight. Now this was a church where you heard people referred to as "babes in Christ," "baby Christians," and "new believers." The effective connotation was that new believers are to be taught and led, but like all babies, they are not able to do anything very complicated.

These people forgot that spiritual babes can be very mature otherwise, and much of the work the Church needs to have done does not require spiritual heavyweights. Both our secular work and our church work require servants with skills in all areas of living. Here I was a new Christian who brought with me many proven talents, yet in the eyes of these men I had none until I was no longer "a babe."

People forget that there is one thing about babies, — they are hungry all the time. Not only are new believers hungry to learn all about God, they are also hungry to do something for God. Almost all want to work for the Lord. These "babes" should not be preachers or deacons right away, or govern the church, but they can work on projects that fit their talent or skills. A key to having fruit that remains is getting new believers involved and doing something right away. *John 15:16* This new responsibility will also help them grow.

When I sensed God closing the door on ministry in my local church, God led me to become a member of the board of directors of a local parachurch organization. I was the only businessman on that board. They wanted a businessman to help them in the functions of management (plan, organize, lead, staff, control, climate-set). I spent more than 20 hours a week for seven years helping bring professional management to the organization.

Do as I did! Go with the skills, gifts, and strengths that you have. Ask God's leading and the Holy Spirit will guide you. Remember God already planned for you to do good works when you were saved. *Ephesians 2:10* These are the abilities that you brought with you from before salvation. Use your experience as your ministry to believers and the lost. By the way, after I had been working on the parachurch board for about a year my church leadership asked me to start a singles ministry (I was single at the time). My daughter Cheri, and I started the ministry, which became the largest door for new members coming into our church. I also ran two separate and successful land acquisition programs. Once they saw me working for the Lord, church leadership knew I was serious and involved me more in the church.

A recent Gallop poll says that if kids get involved in charity work by the age of eleven remaining in charity work the rest of their lives is almost assured. This can be true of new believers as well if they get involved in some ministry soon after their conversion.

A recent survey by respected Christian pollster George Barna says that as little as ten percent of Christians actually do the work in the local church. Why? One reason is because people are not put to work fast enough. Then most become discouraged and lose their inspiration or desire to help. They come to believe that they are not welcome. The church needs to immediately put new believers to work doing things that Christ clearly has called them to do — caregiving. Many caregiving ministries require only a giving heart and a bit of time; not a degree in theology.

1 Corinthians 12:7-10 says, *A spiritual gift is given to each of us as a means of helping the entire* church. To one person the Spirit gives the ability to give wise advice; to another He gives the gift of special knowledge. The Spirit gives special faith to another, and to someone else He gives the power to heal the sick. He gives one person the power to perform miracles, and to another the ability to prophesy. He gives someone else the ability to know whether it is really the Spirit of God or another spirit that is speaking. Still another person is given the ability to speak in unknown languages, and another is given the ability to interpret what is being said. It is the one and only Holy Spirit that distributes these gifts. He alone decides which gift each person should have.

Because many people want some sort of tool to help them clarify their gifts this book includes a spiritual gift inventory you may want to use to help identify your strength areas. Take special note that these type tests are designed by man and are not necessarily inspired by God. They point out your tendencies, which you should check out with family and friends unless you immediately and instinctively agree with the test findings. Discover the spiritual gift God has given you, and then put your gift to use for His Kingdom! Your instincts will tell you if you have chosen properly. If not, look again. (See Appendix A "Discover Your Gifts")

God has given gifts to each of you from his great variety of spiritual gifts. Manage them well so that God's generosity can flow through you. Are you called to be a speaker? Then speak as though God himself were speaking through you. Are you called to help others? Do it with all the strength and energy that God supplies. Then God will be given glory in everything through Jesus Christ. All glory and power belong to Him forever and ever. Amen. *1 Peter 4:10-11*

When you feel that God cannot use you because you are not a professional theologian — remember Paul was the only professional theologian among the Apostles and look what they accomplished. Babes in Christ have a ministry too!

As you do your ministry you don't need to be afraid to witness. You may not be able to define complex theological terms like redemption, justification, and propitiation, but you can still be an effective witness about what Jesus has done in your life. Unbelievers need the simple gospel- that Jesus died for their sin and that they must accept Him by faith. Simply put, because you know the way, you can show others the way. Only one road leads to heaven and Jesus Christ is the way. (See Appendix B)

> You do not have to cross the seas
> Nor foreign lands explore
> To share God's Word with needy souls —
> You'll find them right next door.
> -Anonymous

Personal Perspective Questions
1. At this point do you have a ministry in mind?
2. How much Bible knowledge do you need before you begin?
3. How are you discouraging "babes in Christ" from ministering?
4. What has been given to you? Why was it given? *1 Corinthians 12:7*
5. What is the barrier(s) that is keeping you from getting involved in your ministry "now?"
6. How do you plan to make the most significant difference for God in your lifetime?
7. Does your local church encourage new believers to do good works? If so, would this book be helpful to them?
8. Does your church have a program for putting new believers to work? Can you be an encouragement to others who want to do some sort of ministry?
9. In *Revelation 2:2-5* Jesus speaks to the church of Ephesus. What things are they doing that please Him? What complaint(s) does He have? How can you be encouraged by this scripture?

Group Discussion Questions
1. What is a babe in Christ? *I Peter 2:2*
2. Why do we discourage "babes in Christ" from ministering?
3. According to *John 15:16* God did two things: He "chose" and "appointed". Why?
4. How can we encourage "babes in Christ" ? To serve? To grow? *I Peter 2:2* What can they do?
5. How do these verses clarify "babes in Christ"? *Matthew 11:25, 1 Corinthians 3:1, Hebrews 5:13*
6. According to *1 John 3:22* what pleases God?

YOUR MINISTRY... anything you do to strengthen others!

8. List some tasks needed in your church or community. What Bible knowledge would a "babe in Christ" need before they could help to accomplish these tasks?
9. Does the Bible have spiritual qualifications for Christians to do good works?
10. What do you say when someone says, "I want to help but I'm afraid that I do not know enough."?
11. What does doing for others what they cannot do for themselves really mean?

**YOU CAN MAKE A SIGNIFICANT DIFFERENCE FOR ETERNITY...
YOU CAN DO IT NOW!**

CHAPTER FOUR

WHAT WILL OUR WORKS LOOK LIKE?

Christian lay people number in the millions and can be a giant force for good. We need to wake up that giant.

Let's just stop and think a little about things that you have done to show love to your parents. As a child, I remember going into the woods and picking a handful of wild violets for my mother. As a parent, I remember my kids drawing me pictures as a gift. Now, my grandchildren draw pictures as a sign of their affection. During my cancer recovery, my grandchildren each brought me a picture they had drawn. The pictures meant so much to me that I had them professionally framed. Now if these actions honor us then surely God, our Father, will be equally honored by the meager works we do for Him.

Nothing is too small to bring. *Zechariah 4:10* With Christians there are no secular caregiving works. They are all sacred. From a sacred point of view, cutting a widow's lawn is of as much value as teaching a Sunday school class. *Work hard and cheerfully in whatever you do, as if you are working for the Lord rather than people. Remember that the Lord will give you an inheritance as your reward, and the Master you are serving is Christ. Colossians 3:23-24 Whatever you eat or drink or whatever you do, you must do all for the glory of God. 1 Corinthians 10:31* Martin Luther said that a milk maiden's job or a preacher's job were of equal worth to God. Your ministry, whatever it is, is your witness for Christ — Wow!

It is vitally important that believers find some sort of involvement in a ministry where they can use their particular gifts, experience, and/or skills. *Romans 12:5-8.* But what does that mean? Are you an accountant—then why not help members of your church plan for their retirement? Maybe you could teach "Handling Your Money" classes for singles and newlyweds in the congregation. Or how about helping those in the church who are in financial difficulty to control their credit card usage? You have abilities and wisdom that are needed now. You can have a ministry now. You don't have to wait until you have memorized 50 scripture verses or have been discipled for three years.

Are you an office manager? Maybe you have a gift for organizing events. How about organizing the food drive for Thanksgiving giveaways? Are you a carpenter or car mechanic? Then volunteering to help with the Widows and Orphans Provision Team, which provides home repairs and car care clinics, would be a good idea. Do you have a knack for fixing things? One of the biggest problems for widows is finding someone to do simple fix-it jobs. Are you a sports enthusiast or middle school teacher? Working with the youth group basketball team or tutoring kids who cannot read would be great. The point is to get to work — now.

At times leadership may not have a need for your kind of help. However, there may be individuals in the congregation who do. Your skills in investing and handling money could make you the perfect person to help that newlywed couple you sit next to each Sunday. Your caring about older people could be the answer to a widow's prayer to get to the doctor's office or to church every Sunday.

A friend tells an interesting story. One Sunday, about six months after she was saved, her pastor was teaching on tithing. Because her husband did not understand the importance of giving money to the church, she sat in the pew asking the Lord for a way she could give of her time instead. She wanted nothing more than to give to the Lord because of all He had done for her. After the service, she found herself talking with an elderly woman in a wheelchair. This woman was upset because the person who drove her to church wasn't able to do so any more. She was stunned that God would answer prayer so quickly and clearly. She could do nothing less than become the elderly woman's driver. She became much more over time— washing this woman's clothes, perming her hair and even organizing her funeral when she went on to be with the Lord. My friend felt privileged to do this — because she was ministering and being a witness for God.

Something all believers have in common is 24 hours a day. That's about the extent of our common characteristics other than we are saved by grace. How we use our time is important to God.

One area of spiritual life with which most Christians are not satisfied is their daily devotions. The three components of daily devotions are Bible Study, Meditation, and Prayer. All three are necessary for the spiritual person. Core Ministries' *The Liberating Devotional* is a good way to accomplish balanced daily devotions. (See Appendix C for more information.)

One final thought on the spiritual person: it has not been hard for me to give money to a worthy cause. I give tithes and offerings without difficulty. However, I admit I have never really given "the widow's mite." *Luke 21:2-4* I prayed, meditated, and studied scripture to see just how I could consistently give sacrificially to the Lord. The answer was for me to tithe my time. There are 168 hours in a week. If you take away 56 hours for sleep (God created rest also) — you have 112 productive hours remaining. I began dedicating a minimum of 12 hours a week to worship, prayer, Bible study, charity work, the counseling of other believers, and any other thing that involved kingdom work for which I was not getting paid. For me, my time is "the widow's mite." You have heard success defined as "the feeling you get when you reach a goal, an objective, or solve a problem." I have been tithing my time for over 10 years now, and I feel successful in my walk with the Lord.

Family men and women with young children may say, "There is no way I can do that because of my career demands and the needs of a growing family."

Please consider what a typical week of tithing your time might look like:

- Twenty minutes a day on The Liberating Devotional totals about two and a half hours a week.
- Preparation, travel, and attendance at church and Sunday School on Sunday morning takes three to four hours.
- Sunday night service adds another two hours.
- Midweek small study group or corporate church service involves another two to three hours.
- Preparation for and having family Bible study once a week tacks on an additional two to three hours.
- Prayer for five minutes each night at bedtime increases your time by another half hour.

The above adds up to 14 hours for the week. Still there is choir practice or a Bible study on Thursday morning for another two hours, plus working at the local rescue mission or cutting the widow's yard next door. You see, it really isn't that hard to tithe your time to the Lord. Work out your own "time-tithing budget"-you won't be sorry! Remember, if it is for the Lord the time counts! Now, why not start with 8 hours a week as your target?

By the way, our biggest enemy in staying spiritual is materialism. Materialism means becoming so involved in "the cares of this world" that we do not maintain a walk with God, nor have a relationship with Christ. The Bible reminds us that getting so involved in the things of this world will cause us to become unfruitful. *Matthew 13:22*

Sometimes you will have to look to find an area of ministry. Like myself, some people will find their place of service either in a Christian charity organization or some community institution. For example, you can look outside the local body of Christ to a nursing home, crisis pregnancy center, or rescue mission. We are called to be salt and light to the world. *Matthew 5:13-16* We have to get out of the shaker and up on a lamp stand to accomplish that.

Ephesians 4:12 says that each of us has a ministry — a work (see also *Ephesians 2:10*). In *Mark 13:34*, Jesus says that every man has his work. In other words, God has a work for you. You need to take the initiative to accomplish that work to His glory and with the support of your local church leaders. Please realize that God has already gifted you for your ministry!

YOUR MINISTRY... anything you do to strengthen others!

In *1 Peter 4* we read about God's grace flowing through the believer to others. Grace is undeserved favor — the free kindness that comes from the Lord. Grace is God's presence in our lives to empower us to be what He wants us to be in order to do what He wants us to do. We experience His grace, not only as the favor of His forgiveness, but also as the energy and ability He gives to help us live the way He wants us to.

Accepting and using this gift brings blessings to you and to others, and it honors the name and kindness of the giver. Peter urged his readers to use and express God's grace by being watchful in their prayers, showing love, being hospitable, and ministering to others. Remember that the only limit to God's grace is the limit we put on it by resisting His presence in our lives.

> No service in itself is small,
> None great, though earth it fill;
> But that is small that seeks its own,
> And great that does God's will.
> — Anonymous

Today one of the biggest problems with those who are doing ministry in and out of the church is that they are doing it in their own strength and ability. The result is business without spiritual fruit; people get discouraged, frustrated, quit, etc.. How do you make sure that you are not doing ministry in your own strength, but Christ's? *2 Peter 1:3-11* tells us that as we know Christ better His divine power will give us everything we need to live a Godly life. The secret is knowing Jesus better...spending time reading His Word *2 Timothy 2:15, James 1:22-27* and praying. We should build our life on His Word and build His Word into our life. This is how we will get our marching orders. As you read on in *2 Peter 1:1-11,* you will see the steps toward growing a genuine love for everyone. This love will manifest itself in a caregiving ministry. Another reason we get frustrated and discouraged in ministry is that we don't leave the results up to God. Perhaps we need to redefine what being God's servant really is. In human terms a servant asks the master what needs to be done and then proceeds to do it. The Bible describes God's servant as someone who God works through. The human servant is responsible to listen to his master's commands and for the results. God's servant is responsible to be faithful to God's commands but the results are God's. God wants to work through us *John 5:19, John 15:5* and we will succeed if we let Him.

When my twins were three years old, my son Tom brought me a balloon that had just popped.

He said, "Daddy fix," just like he usually did when I came home from work and one of his toys had broken. In the past I had always been able to fix the problem — but a broken balloon? I wished that we had a spare balloon to give Tom, but we didn't. I told Tom I could not fix it. Tom looked at me for a moment and then said, "Daddy fix." I proceeded with the explanation that some things even Daddy cannot fix. Well, when I finally got the point across to Tom, you should have seen the look in his eyes. His champion was not a champion any longer. Many of you had to go through something similar with your own dad. But today we know a Father we call Abba *Romans 8:15* who can do everything, and He is the one to whom we take our broken balloons. This story is told to make the point that your expectations of others should not be like young Tom. In caregiving ministry you do your best to fix what is damaged, and then, give over the popped balloons to God. Remember, as good stewards you are called to be faithful. *1 Corinthians 4:1-2* The success part is God's job.

A few years ago I wrote the first in a series of books to be used in prison ministry. Much time was spent on research and the results were very pleasing. The first book was called *Inside Brother's Check-Up.* Before the book went to press my wife Linda and I were returning from northern Michigan when she startled me by asking, "What about the inmates who cannot read?" I recalled what Jesus said about feeding the poor, and that He also said that the poor would always be with us. My conclusion was that we are to feed the poor that we can, but we will not be able to feed them all. I told Linda that the prisoners who can read would just have to help those who could not read.

It is easy to recall the frustration at how slowly the *Inside Brother's Check-Up* took off. It had been field-tested and received the enthusiastic endorsement from every major Christian prison ministry that I could find. Yet, the books just trickled out. My pastor kept telling me that God calls us to be faithful, not successful; but in my heart I wanted to be successful. It always has been hard leaving the results to God.

When we decide to obey God, it's easy for most of us to assume that life, and especially our ministry, will go smoothly. When all is well with life and ministry, we think it proves that we are in God's will. When we are facing difficulty and setbacks, we may conclude that our work is out of God's will. Rather than questioning our measurement or interpretation, we question our dedication, and sometimes even God.

It is a mistake to believe that if we obey God, everything will go well. Being dedicated to God means going with Him even when things go wrong from our perspective. In fact, He said assuredly that the gospel advances on disaster and suffering. Read *Philippians 1:12-18.* Never forget, we are called to be faithful. *1 Corinthians 4:1-2* Success is God's job!

Once in a while great things happen. Core Ministries' jail and prison program has grown to where it publishes a quarterly newspaper called *The Christian Inmate News.* This paper is sent to 100,000 men, women and youth inmates in every state and federal prison, and 600 of the largest jails in the USA. It is truly a trans-denominational publication. It is positive and has a goal of helping to get out the life-changing message of Jesus Christ along with preparing the inmates for successful transition into civilian life — so that when they get out they stay out. (Remember 98% are going to be released.)

Although I write some of the articles, the most unique thing about *The Christian Inmate News* is that it is written mostly by Christian inmates *for* Christian inmates. Its impact is awesome, and it began with acting upon the desire to help. The Holy Spirit placed the desire upon my heart. In a way, it is allowing some Christian inmates to minister using their past experiences. It is a caregiving ministry for them.

A Tale of Three Families and Their Ministries (Passions):

Josh & Dottie

In 1984 I became friends with Josh & Dottie McDowell. Their passions are many, but their work with teenagers and parents of teenagers is second to none. I was involved in their wonderful ministry until 1990 when my wife and I started Core Ministries. (One thing missing since starting Core is that I no longer have the time to be involved with Josh & Dottie's ministry. Perhaps we will work together again; if not here on earth then after.) Josh and Dottie both helped launch Core Ministries. Josh endorsed many of my books and has written the forward to my biggest work, *The Teens Clinic.* Dottie helped me by co-authoring a great resource called *Mom's Check Up.* Through this close association with the McDowells my observation is that their ministry is a partnership of equal passion.

Dave & Linda

My wife, Linda, has always been supportive of my involvement with Core Ministries — both professionally and financially. She is also the final editor of all Core materials. We, too, have a partnership of equal passion in the same ministry. This will not be true with all spouses. Some

spouses may have separate or distinct ministries. This is the case with my daughter Cheri and her husband Mark.

Mark & Cheri

Cheri's husband Mark has one of the most beautiful singing voices I have ever heard. He loves to serve the Lord by providing special music at Sunday worship services. This is his ministry. Though Cheri's ability to handle the responsibilities at home helps Mark's ministry by giving him the time needed to practice and perform at multiple services — it is still not her passion. After talking with my daughter at one of our monthly father-daughter lunch meetings, she discovered where her passion lies. She has always had a sensitivity toward helping others find their niche — helping women who are new to a neighborhood, church, or school and networking them in such a way that they will soon be productive members of that group. The result is twofold: they are no longer feeling like outsiders, and they are helping to serve others in the process. This is a win-win situation and is the focus of much of Cheri's ministry work today.

Remember, a ministry can be so many different things. A person can have a different ministry from their spouse, they can partner with their spouse in ministry, or they can have a family ministry (involving their kids). They can even have a combination of the above. There are no limits on what you can do to help serve the Lord. The important thing is that you find a passion and pursue it.

The numbers reached by Josh and Dottie's ministries are hundreds of thousands every year. Dave and Linda's ministry affect tens of thousands. Mark's ministry impacts hundreds; and Cheri's ministry may help 20 or more. Core Ministries is twice removed from those they try to help, while Cheri's ministry is up front and personal. God is equally pleased with all of our ministries. To Him it is not a game of numbers, but rather making the best of whatever gifts and opportunities He has given us. Unlike the world, God looks at our motives and our obedience in serving Him and others. He doesn't measure our success by quantitative measures, but by our heart.

Another point to remember is that there are seasons to our life. Our ministries often change with these seasons. Our time, resources, and passions will change with our life's circumstances. Don't get discouraged if you have a passion for a ministry that you are unable to accomplish now. You can continue to pray about it. There may come a day when you will have the time, resources, health, etc. for it. Or God will give you a passion for something else. The seasons start with the young and extend to the very old. *Even children are known by the way they act... Proverbs 20:11* so even children and teens learn to be givers. Then, there are the retired and elderly that can find a way to remain fruitful. *Even in old age they will still produce fruit; they will remain vital and green. Psalm 92:14*

When Cheri had toddlers at home and a traveling husband, she had little time for anything else. What could she do at that stage? She prayed and the Lord brought neighborhood children to her door to minister to during that season of her life. When Josh and Dottie's children were young, Dottie's primary ministry was that of raising her four youngsters. Dottie took care of the home front so that Josh could carry on his demanding calling in the ministry, which involved him being away from home a large portion of the time. Now that their children have grown, Dottie's role has changed, and she is more involved in the specific details of the ministry. Does she play a more important role now in the ministry than before? Absolutely not — it was her help and support that allowed Josh his vast accomplishments. Both roles are vitally important.

Time doesn't always permit us to work, have a ministry outside the home, and spend adequate time raising a godly family. If this is where you are right now, then your family is your main ministry. Make sure to commit this to fervent prayer though, because often times God may have a ministry in store for us that won't take away from the family, but may involve the family members working together. Most of family neglect circumstances aren't from choices between family and a single ministry, but rather, people who have chosen involvement in multiple ministries at the expense of their family. Be sure not to overcommit. No one can be involved in every good ministry. Therefore, we must make choices and let others fill in where we can't.

As we serve God, we must attempt to do some part of the massive work He has called His Church to do. You cannot do it all. Not being able to do everything should not prevent us from doing something. The key is to start to do the work and let the results be His. You have a ministry. If you don't know where to begin, start by making your passion your ministry. Wake the giant in you and start today! Christian lay-people number in the millions and can be a giant force for good. We need to wake up that giant!

YOUR MINISTRY... ANYTHING YOU DO TO STRENGTHEN OTHERS!

Personal Perspective Questions

1. Are you worthless or insignificant to God? *Zechariah 4:10*
2. According to *Matthew 5:13-16* what does God call Christians? What is your "light?"
3. Do you have abilities and wisdom that are needed now? Do you have a ministry now?
4. Has God already gifted you for your ministries? (Remember *Ephesians 2:10*)
5. What did Dorcas do in *Acts 9:36,39* that you can also do?
6. What impact did Dorcas' acts of kindness have on others? Do you ever see your potential acts of kindness as trivial in the kingdom?
7. What is your greatest strength and can it be used for good works?
8. In *Mark 13:32-37* what was Jesus warning us about? How does this apply to you? Can you "fix" everything?" What does God call us to do? *1 Corinthians 4:2*
9. Of what comfort is it to know your responsibility is to be faithful not successful?
10. Why is it hard to leave the results to God?
11. How faithful are you to your family? Have you remembered to balance your ministry with your family?
12. Can your family have a ministry that will bring them together instead of dividing them? What good work could you do together with your family?
13. In *Matthew 11:29-30* Jesus says *"Take my yoke upon you. Let me teach you, because I am humble and gentle, and you will find rest for your souls. For my yoke fits perfectly, and the burden I give you is light"*. What is this rest that Jesus promises? Does it mean the end of work?
14. How does a relationship with God change meaningless, weariness toil into spiritual productivity and purpose?

Group Discussion Questions

1. Why do we seek to separate the secular from the sacred?
2. What does *Colossians 3:23* and *1 Corinthians 10:31* tell us?
3. How should our work habits and attitudes on our job differ from our ministry? How can we minister to others at work? What things shouldn't be done during work hours?
4. How can we encourage people to use their gifts, experience, and abilities — within the church —outside the church? What things might we be doing to discourage them?
5. How can we encourage others to "bring what you have?"
6. Is it possible to limit God's grace? If so, what are common ways we limit God's grace?
7. Grace is God's presence in our lives to empower us to be what He wants us to be in order to do what He wants us to do. How does this work in our church? In us?
8. What criteria do you think God will use when you are called to give an account of your life? *2 Corinthians 5:10* Are the good works that Christians do pleasing to God?
9. Do believers have a role in encouraging others to do good works? *Hebrews 10: 25*
10. Why does God not call us to be successful?
11. Why do we place so much attention on numbers?
12. How do we achieve a balance between family and ministry?
13. What do you say when someone says, "I want to help but I have to take care of my family."
14. How can the whole family be involved in a ministry? Give examples.
15. Can a church, family, individual try to do too much? Because one can't do everything... can saying "no" to a ministry thwart God's plan?
16. Are there some who can do more or less than others? — Singles, wealthy, etc. ...
17. There are different seasons to ministry involvement...young mothers, retirees; give examples of other seasons.
18. Does it make sense for parents of young children to get involved in the ministries focused on their children?
19. What ministries would be good in other stages of life? Give examples.
20. Using the definition *Your Ministry...Anything You Do to Strengthen Others*! — brainstorm at least 50 things that qualify as ministry.
21. According to *Ephesians 4:7-8* Christ gave us what special gift?

YOU CAN MAKE A SIGNIFICANT DIFFERENCE FOR ETERNITY... YOU CAN DO IT NOW!

Caution: There needs to be balance in everything we do! One problem often seen in the church is that individuals place church responsibilities ahead of family. It seems that they sometimes forget that we are responsible to our family's needs first before we look outside the home for a ministry. For example, our most important ministry as parents is to raise Godly children. The Lord commands us to take care of our family. *1 Timothy 5:8*

TIME IS SLIPPING AWAY

You make your bed on earth and sleep on it in heaven (or somewhere else).

Our time is a depreciating asset. It goes by no matter how we use it. Most of us act as if that number is so great that it may as well be infinite. That's just not true! Consider that:

- 25 years is 9,125 days
- 15 years is 5,475 days
- 5 years is 1,825 days

Therefore, teach us to number our days. *Psalm 90:12*

Now some of us have thousands of days left on earth and others have only hundreds, or less. This was brought home to me in 1995 after seven months and over 40 appointments with eight doctors for severe pain in my left shoulder, when the eighth doctor found something. He said, "You have something terrible going on inside your body. The good news is that I can save your arm. The bad news is I must remove your shoulder."

The doctor diagnosed a rare bone cancer called chondrosarcoma which does not respond to chemotherapy or radiation. The only chance for survival was total removal of every cancer cell. What a jolt that news was! At the time I was using *Our Daily Bread* in my devotions and the next day's key verse was *2 Corinthians 5:8. Yes, we are fully confident, and we would rather be away from these bodies, for then we will be at home with the Lord.* I thought that maybe it was my time. Facing this situation made every minute with family, friends, and co-workers much more meaningful.

The operation was a success — they cut away the cancer. They saved the arm, but all that is holding it on is skin, blood vessels, and nerves. I do have some use of my hand; which means I am able to work fairly well at a computer keyboard. This is what I do most of the time in my job. The successful operation allowed me to write this book. I thank God periodically for the spell-checker as I often hit the wrong keys. I also tell my wife how sad I am that dishes and yard work are out of the question. (She doesn't believe me!)

Stop for a minute and make believe you, too, have just been told you have cancer. How would you look at your life then? What would it do to your world-view? What changes would you make today?

I am so grateful that I am still here, because I feel the Lord has more work for me to do. However, if I had died, I would now be present with the Lord; and that would be great! I like what my mother says about dying. She says that she's ready to go, she just hasn't bought the ticket yet. I want to stay here as long as God will use me; plus it will be fun to see my grandchildren grow up. *Philippians 1:19-26*

Coming so close to death has intensified my view of heaven and my time left here on earth. *Hebrews 9:27* tells us that it is destined that each person dies only once and after that comes judgment. But what will that judgment look like?

Visualize going to be with the Lord as follows: The first event will be to stand before the Judgment Seat of Christ. Christians will be judged to see if we get rewards or not. *For we must all stand before Christ to be judged. We will each receive whatever we deserve for the good or evil we have done in our bodies. 2 Corinthians 5:10* Call this the Judgment Seat of Christ or the "24 hour seat" because how we use each 24 hours is what will be considered there—and will determine our rewards in heaven.

> **To review:**
> 1. We are saved by grace through faith and not works. *Ephesians 2:5,8,9*
> 2. After we are saved, we are told to go to work. *Ephesians 2:10*
> 3. We are judged by our works as to what rewards we get in heaven — this occurs at the "24 hour seat". *Matthew 16:27; 2 Corinthians 5:10; Revelation 22:12* (Keep in mind that motives are very important here.)
> 4. Once we die our eternal destiny is locked — not only where we spend eternity, but also what rewards we will receive. There is nothing more we can do but accept God's judgments. *Luke 16:22-23 (19-31)*

We go into such detail about this because it is important for you to know that what you do now with your time matters for eternity. Another way of saying this is "You make your bed on earth and sleep on it in heaven (or somewhere else)."

Once we realize how temporary this life is (like the cancer scare showed me) we appreciate that we may be meeting the Lord sooner rather than later. For some of us there may not be a lot more time left to affect how we will spend eternity. How we spend eternity hinges on our life now. Notice it does not say "where" but "how." Think about it, a street sweeper in heaven is infinitely better off than a ruler in hell. Jesus speaks often enough about rewards that it is appropriate to desire them. *Matthew 5:12; 6:1; 10:41; 16:27; Luke 6:23; 6:35* We want to hear the Lord say to us, *"Well done, good and faithful servant." Matthew 25:21*

In summary, what we do each day matters for eternity. This is powerful! To repeat, our job, along with things like being a parent and a spouse — as well as our works of Christian charity, all matter for eternity.

You need to be doing ministry. It can be spontaneous or planned. It can be within your church or without. You can be involved in a large ministry or be working on your own. Your work can be done with other Christians or not. The point is that each of us needs to be doing ministry. Together we are a giant and it is time to wake up! We all have a ministry and the clock is ticking!

THE HANDS OF TIME   *By Bobby E. Rogers*

There is only one thing in life on earth that cannot be stopped ... The hands of time, the ticking of the clock...

As the days come and go, and the seasons continue to change ...

I realize that something is wrong in my life, and it's time to rearrange...

I've tried every way that I thought I knew how. Only to end up, where I am now...

So much time has past, and how expensive the cost, The price that I paid "as the sheep that was lost".

My worries are now over, for I am no longer lost, but found... From our Heavenly Father, who created us from the dust of the ground...

He sent His only begotten Son to die for our sins, Not just for you and me, but also our family and friends...

To have an eternal life of Joy, and escape from the ticking of the clock, "Repent and accept Jesus Christ" as Lord and Savior, And return to the "Heavenly Flock."

Amen.

Core Ministries publishes quarterly *The Christian Inmate News* which features writings of inmates. This poem from a recent issue is appropriate for this chapter.

Personal Perspective Questions

1. How long will you live? *Psalm 31:15, John 21:22*
2. What would you do differently today, if you knew you would die tomorrow? Next week? Next month? Next year?
3. What happens after death? *Hebrews 9:27*
4. What should you do with your time? *Psalm 90:12*
5. How would God define "making the most of your time"? How much would His definition differ from the world's view?
6. Why does what you do now matter for eternity? *Matthew 16:27*
7. Are you acutely aware of your earthly mortality?
8. Have you considered that only what you have done for Christ can go with you when you die?
9. If Jesus asked you to give up everything and follow him — what would be the hardest thing to give up? *Matthew 19:21-22*

Group Discussion Questions

1. Read *Matthew 25:31-46.* What does this passage tell us concerning the work we should be doing? Name the work and how to do it — what are the consequences of obeying or disobeying?
2. How does this passage encourage us to work?
3. The Bible tells us that time is slipping away. How does it tell us to act? *Romans 13:11-14*
4. Did you ever see a U-Haul trailer hooked to the back of a hearse? What are you storing in your U-Haul that you can't take with you?
5. Consider this quote from Jim Elliott, " He is no fool who gives what he cannot keep to gain what he cannot lose." What does it mean to you?
6. Is it always bad to store up treasures on earth? (401-K, life insurance, mutual funds, annuities and the like)

YOUR MINISTRY... anything you do to strengthen others!

CHAPTER SIX

THE REWARD PARADOX – OR IS IT?

In the final analysis it is about pleasing God rather than building rewards in heaven.

We have all heard people say that if you do a good deed and people find out about it — it doesn't count. Jesus said, *"You are the light of the world — like a city on a mountain, glowing in the night for all to see. Don't hide your light under a basket! Instead, put it on a stand and let it shine for all. In the same way, let your good deeds shine out for all to see, so that everyone will praise your heavenly Father."* Matthew 5:14-16 **(emphasis mine)** Then He said, *"Take care! Don't do your good deeds publicly, to be admired, because then you will lose the reward from your Father in heaven. When you give a gift to someone in need, don't shout about it as the hypocrites do — blowing trumpets in the synagogues and streets to call attention to their acts of charity! I assure you, they have received all the reward they will ever get. But when you give to someone, don't tell your left hand what your right hand is doing. Give your gifts in secret, and your Father, who knows all secrets, will reward you."* Matthew 6:1-4 **(emphasis mine)**

After reading these passages ask yourself a few questions:
1. Why is it bad to get rewards here and now?
2. How important is it to let our light shine?
3. How is doing God's will reward enough?
4. Is what we're doing motivated by our heart to please God or our ego to please ourselves?

When I first became a believer I did my best to be a good steward of the funds God had given me. My business background made it crystal clear that if a charity were IRS approved I could deduct donations on my income tax. This way I could give more money to charities. For example I paid 39% federal and 4.6% state income tax. If I wanted to give an IRS approved charity $1,000, it cost $1,000 out of my income. But if I wanted to give $1,000 to a nondeductible charity, it cost $1,773 out of my income because I had to pay taxes first. This was a pretty dramatic difference, so I went to great lengths to give to approved charities; that way I could give more to God's work. (The extra came from the taxes I did not have to pay.)

This was all well and good, but I began to come across fellow believers that were not IRS approved charities; yet had real needs that I could fill. My "good steward mindset" kept getting in the way; I thought this was not the best use of my charity budget. After much prayer and consideration, I realized that it was God's will at times for me to give according to the need, rather than the tax consequences. In other words go ahead and pay the taxes and give what's left where the need is.

In a similar fashion, it is sometimes appropriate to do works publicly and forgo the reward in heaven. Matthew 6:1-4 In the final analysis it is about pleasing God rather than building rewards in heaven. Just being in heaven is enough. God looks at our heart and not the outward appearances. Our goal is to do the right thing in God's eyes and not worry what the world says or does. Aim to please God and don't worry about the rest!

Consider this prayer Saint Paul prayed for the church at Colossi. *So we have continued praying for you ever since we first heard about you. We ask God to give you a complete understanding of what He wants to do in your lives, and we ask Him to make you wise with spiritual wisdom. Then the way you live will always honor and please the Lord, and you will continually do good, kind things for others. All the while, you will learn to know God better and better.* Colossians 1:9-10 Simply put, give in a way that brings glory to God and not yourself. *1 Corinthians 10:31*

Personal Perspective Questions
1. It is important to let your light shine. Matthew 5:14-16 Can you give a specific example of what that means in everyday life?
2. From whom would you rather receive a reward — men or God? Matthew 6:19-21
3. What do *Matthew 25:14-30* and *1 Corinthians 4:2* teach you?
4. Do you lose your heavenly reward if someone praises you for your good works?
5. Can you please man and God at the same time?
6. Think of good deeds you are currently doing. Ask yourself if what you're doing is motivated by your heart to please God or your ego to please yourself?
7. Do you look for rewards now or later? Matthew 6:1-21

Group Discussion Questions

1. According to *Matthew 5:14-15*, how are we to do our good deeds?
2. According to *Matthew 6:1-4*, how are we not to do our good deeds?
3. How can we teach others to be better servants? Givers of charitable gifts?
4. What is meant by "forgo my reward in Heaven"? *Matthew 6:1-4*
5. Is the promise of a heavenly reward for doing a good deed our only motivation? What others?
6. Should we keep track of our good deeds? Why?
7. Should we praise others for good deeds? Why?
8. One of the greatest benefits we get here on earth from serving God is the privilege, knowledge, and joy that He can use you and me. What other benefits can you think of that a person gets from serving God?

The following reprint of a page out of *Our Daily Bread* sums it up best.

SATURDAY - JANUARY 19   READ: MATTHEW 6:19-24

BOTH GLAD AND SAD

**Do not lay up for yourselves treasures on earth ...
but ... treasures in heaven. - Matthew 6:19,20**

There's an old legend about three men who were crossing a desert on horseback during the night. As they approached a dried-up creek bed, they heard a voice commanding them to stop and dismount, pick up some pebbles, put them in their pockets, and not look at them until the next morning. The men were also promised that if they obeyed they would be both glad and sad. After they did as they were told, the three mounted their horses and went on their way.

As the first gray streaks of dawn began to spread across the eastern sky, the men reached into their pockets to pull out the pebbles. To their great surprise, they had been transformed into diamonds, rubies, and other precious gems. It was then that they realized the significance of the promise that they would be both glad and sad. They were happy that they had picked up as many pebbles as they did, but sorry - so sorry - that they had not collected more.

You will no doubt feel something like that when you get to heaven. You will be happy for the treasure you laid up in heaven while on earth and joyful for the rewards Christ will give us. But you will also experience regret for not having done more to serve Him.

Let's make the most of our opportunities so that we'll be more glad than sad. –
Richard W. DeHaan

*The day will come when you will stand
Before our Judge, God's Son;
Have you so lived that He will say,
"Well done, My child, well done"? - Sper*

THE CROWNS YOU WEAR IN HEAVEN MUST BE WON ON EARTH.

(From "Our Daily Bread" copyright by RBC Ministries, Grand Rapids, MI. Reprinted with permission.)

YOU CAN MAKE A SIGNIFICANT DIFFERENCE FOR ETERNITY...
YOU CAN DO IT NOW!

WHAT CAN YOU DO?

Your mess will become your message and your misery your ministry.

As you have probably figured out by now, this book sees faith as an action word. The role of the Church in the 21st Century, when dealing with the poor and disadvantaged, as both speaking out and going out. Speaking out by proclaiming the good news and going out by taking it to those who are most in need. This fulfills what Jesus said, *"The Spirit of the Lord is upon me, for he has appointed me to preach Good News to the poor. He has sent me to proclaim that captives will be released, that the blind will see, that the downtrodden will be freed from their oppressors, and that the time of the Lord's favor has come." Luke 4:18-19* Should we do any less? James says, Pure and lasting religion in the sight of God our Father means that we must care for orphans and widows in their troubles, and refuse to let the world corrupt us. *James 1:27* The Church in the 21st century must see poverty, illness, addiction, and crime as an opportunity to take God to the those who are hurting.

Why are these areas our greatest opportunity to do caregiving works? Simply because this is where we are called to serve. *Matthew 25:31-46* These people have a pressing need for God. They are often in a place of brokenness and despair. Our country needs the healing message of Christ! There is no other hope.

My area of focus is in criminal justice ministry (CJM). Studies from all over the world agree that the majority of those incarcerated are addicted to alcohol or other drugs (between 60% and 80%). Other studies tell more of the story. The vast majority of violent criminals have no consistent, healthy father-figure in their lives. Many come from lives of poverty and abuse. It is a field ripe for harvest and the workers are few.

Using the word addiction more loosely, there are many more addictions. All are the result of sin (ours or someone else's) and require God's intervention for healing and recovery to take place. Not only do addictions affect the life of the addict practicing them; they can also bring great pain and destruction to the addicted person's family, business, church and community. Review the following list and see if you can discover an area of caregiving ministry that touches your heart. It may be to the addicted person or to those whose lives are affected by the addict. It may be that you were once troubled by one of the addictions on the list. Maybe it was your father, mother, sister, brother, husband, wife or child that was struggling. Through God's grace in the midst of your experiences you have learned much that can help others become whole. You become what is called a wounded-healer. Being healed by God, you can now help those who are afflicted. "He comforts us in all our troubles so that we can comfort others. When others are troubled, we will be able to give them the same comfort God has given us." *2 Corinthians 1:4*

A Few Possible Addictions

Alcohol	Illegal drugs
Legal drugs	Food
Pornography	Anger
Sex	Violence
Fame - pride	Work
Power	Control
Shopping	Victimization
Religion	Self-pity
Gossiping	Gambling
Idols of all Kinds	Self-righteousness
Money in All Forms	Internet

Every believer has a mission to accomplish. It may be found in the list on this page. The approach of the Church of the 21st Century should include sending out those wounded-healers to show the love of Christ to those who are still suffering. Wounded-healers have first-hand credible experience to share — this makes them worthy of trust when helping those who suffer the same addiction.

The wounded-healer approach does not just apply to addictions. Wounded-healers are needed as caregivers in areas such as divorce recovery, single parenting, crisis pregnancy, chronic illness, terminal illness, and unemployment. It is God's special grace in each of our lives that makes us particularly suited to minister to others with like circumstance and/or sin. Your 'been there — done that' experience is invaluable. Your mess will become your message and your misery your ministry.

Caution: Please be careful if you are trying to minister in an area with which you're still struggling. In that case you might want to pray for a caregiver yourself and choose a different ministry to do your caregiving in.

Life has many lessons. As we live we make many choices — some good — some bad. The bad choices can wound us and the good reinforce us. Our life experiences make us ideal candidates to mentor others of the same sex. There are verses about men seeking the counsel of older men. *1 Peter 5:1-5* God calls older women in Titus to be mentors to younger women. In her book, *What Every Mother Needs to Know*, Brenda Hunter says, "A woman needs a mentor — someone she admires about 15 to 20 years older who is already well up the mountain she intends to climb. Someone who will say to her 'Come up' the air is wonderful up here." Sometimes she will have to do more than say "Come up" but instead she will have to reach back and help someone with the climb. A mentor can use what she has learned to help others — to prepare God's people for works of service, so that the body of Christ may be built up. *Ephesians 4:12*

So, one caregiving work to consider is mentoring. Younger people of your same sex can benefit greatly from a mentoring relationship with you. We all have our life's experiences we can share. Our contemporary society has created many damaged and confused teens that do not have a healthy father relationship. Men certainly can help here. And look at the many single moms our divorce culture has created. Women can help here. What follows is taken from a section in *Teen's Clinic,* also by this author titled *Mentors: Why Do I Need Them and How Do I Find One?* The article is encouraging teenagers to find a mentor. Turn the advice around for being a mentor and keep in mind that we are encouraged to be both a mentor and a protégé.

Mentoring is not discipleship. Discipleship focuses on spiritual growth. Mentoring focuses on all areas of growth. Discipleship is usually done for a limited time while mentoring is done for a long time, if not a lifetime. While discipleship requires mutual respect, mentoring involves a much deeper bond; a personal chemistry. Discipleship is the teaching of spiritual truths, mentoring is a commitment to involvement in all aspects of your life. It is a powerful, loving, emotionally encouraging relationship that grows with time.

A mentor can be a hero of yours, but he or she is not just a hero figure that you watch from afar. A mentor is more than a role model, more than a coach, is more than a friend, and more than an advisor. The mentoring relationship requires a natural chemistry between mentor and protégé. It is not something that can be assigned by a church leader or school counselor. Those relationships that are assigned may work for a while. Quite possibly, they may grow into something very deep. But often matched relationships produce deep frustration because too much is expected of the bond. Mentors and protégés must like each other, enjoy each other's company, and believe in each other. A mentor must really want to see you win in life and be willing to make the sacrifice of time and emotional energy.

A mentor is not perfect; does not have to be old; and doesn't have to have all the answers. The mentoring process does not involve a curriculum, nor is the main focus of the mentor to hold the protégé accountable. A list of qualities that protégés in Portland, Oregon created includes the following chart titled Qualities of a Mentor.

QUALITIES OF A MENTOR

- Consistent, stable
- Affirming
- Believed in me
- Accepted me where I was at
- Saw me as a person of value
- Included me in their life
- Fun
- A person of character, trustworthy
- I admired the mentor
- There was a naturally positive relationship between us
- I knew my mentor was not perfect-didn't matter

You might think, 'Well why do I need to make this a formal thing? Why can't I just watch those people that I think are special and learn from them at a distance?' It's true that you will learn things that way. However, you will not gain the benefit that is available through a long-term committed relationship that has your success as its main focus. Think for a minute: What if you were in trouble and needed someone to talk to at 2 AM or felt the need to call this person at his or her place of business? Would you feel free to do so? I don't think so. On the other hand, if you were in a mentor/protégé relationship there would already be an understanding about such a call.

You are encouraged to be both a mentor and to find a mentor. I have done this for years and it has given me great satisfaction and help. You can get more information by contacting Bobb Biehl at Masterplanning Group @ 800-443-1976. His book *Mentoring: Confidence in Finding and Being a Mentor* is a good place to start.

Christians are to serve the Lord with all our heart, mind, and strength in whatever area He calls us. We are unique creatures, and God wants to use that uniqueness in His service. Your service may be within your local fellowship, a parachurch organization, out in the world, or any combination of these three. There is a subtle difference in how you approach each area — which is why unity of purpose is important. In other words keep in mind what you are trying to accomplish and stay out of issues that are not necessary to complete your ministry.

Again, if you don't know where you should serve, ask yourself where your compassion is the greatest. What trials has God brought you through so that you may use your experience to help others? If you cannot find some area to minister where your specific experience and talents take you, maybe you need the help of others in knowing your gift. (See Appendix A —Discover your Gifts)

THE IDEAL MENTOR CHECKLIST

1. Honest with you
2. A model for you
3. Deeply committed to you
4. Open and transparent
5. A teacher
6. One who believes in your potential
7. One who can help you define your dream and plan to turn your dream into reality
8. Successful in your eyes
9. Be open to learning from you, as well as teaching you
10. Willing to stay primarily on your agenda, not hers/his

BIBLICAL FOUNDATIONS FOR MENTORING

I Godly counsel is a major theme in the Bible
- A wise person welcomes instruction and reproof. *Proverbs 9:8-9*
- A person who heeds instruction will show others the way of life. *Proverbs 10:17*
- No guidance leads to failure. *Proverbs 11:14*
- A wise person listens to advice. *Proverbs 12:15; 13:10*
- There is poverty and shame if instructions are ignored. *Proverbs 13:18*
- A scoffer will not go to the wise. *Proverbs 15:12*
- Without counsel plans go wrong. *Proverbs 15:22*
- Listen to advice and gain wisdom. *Proverbs 19:20*
- Plans are established by counsel. *Proverbs 20:18*
- Multiple counselors lead to safety. *Proverbs 24:6*

II Accountability is a theme in the Bible
- Many teachings of Jesus illustrate God's standards and intent concerning accountability. *Matthew 18:15-19; 23-35, Matthew 25:14-30, Luke 12: 16-20, and Luke 19:12-26*
- We are to look to the interests of others *Philippians 2:4*, teaching and admonishing one another. *Colossians 3:16*
- Since God will ultimately hold us accountable *Romans 14:12, Matthew 12:36* it would be wise to ask for accountability from fellow believers to keep us on track. *Galatians 6:1*
- Older women are to train younger women to live self-controlled and pure lives. *Titus 2:3-5*
- Paul's teaching to both Timothy and Titus includes instructions to both young and old men to be self-controlled, worthy of respect, men of integrity and sound doctrine. *Titus 2:2 & 6 1; 1 Timothy 3:1-12; 4:6; 5:1*

III Mutual support is Biblical
- The Bible says that anxiety in a person's heart weighs him or her down, but a good word makes him or her glad. *Proverbs 12:25*
- Two working together are better than one, and three are better still. *Ecclesiastes 4:9-12*
- We are encouraged to build one another up. *1 Thessalonians 5:11*
- We are also encouraged to bear one another's burdens *Galatians 6:2*, and to love each other deeply. *1 Peter 4:8*

The Holy Spirit is in us to convict our heart and show us where we are to minister. He knows our gifts! While seeking to understand what area you are best suited to minister, don't forget to pray. Maybe you are truly one of the special ones — a prayer warrior. Your work may be the most important of all. Many believe that it is. Intercessory prayer on my behalf has saved my ministry many times over. As a start you can commit to pray every day for your pastor and the church leadership. Our spiritual leaders are targets of the evil one and need to be covered in prayer. They are human and susceptible to every temptation with which you are tempted. Satan will attack them through their families so pray for their families also. In prayer we are asking God to provide for that person what we can't provide. God gives us the privilege of being involved as a partner in His work of justice, salvation, comfort and healing.

There is a ministry that is presently helping me. It's called the "TGIF Prayer Group." A year ago a group of men that get together Friday mornings for worship decided to devote their time to intercessory prayer for specific people and their needs. They have their own stationary and every week they mail a personalized letter, with a positive message, plus an attachment of some inspirational saying. About six months ago a friend of mine put me on TGIF's list and I have been getting a letter a week ever since. Once a name is put on their list they commit to keep praying during the duration of the need, and in my case it has been ongoing. They ask for feedback and even have an E-mail address so that I can send them specific requests and answers to prayers. Many times when someone on their list goes on to meet the Lord, they continue to pray for the spouse and family to get through the grief. This ministry has meant a lot to me; I live in Michigan. This group is in a church in Central Florida. Currently their list is about 150 people. They certainly will hear, "Well done my good and faithful servant."

Here is one more story about prayer: Six years ago my daughter-in-law, Diane, had to quit her job because of illness. Since then she has been to such renowned places as the Mayo Clinic and the Ann Arbor Pain Clinic. She has seen at least ten specialists but to no avail. She has been sick more time than she has been well. In the past year she had deteriorated to where her quality of life was at a minimum. A few months ago she was rushed to emergency because of a reaction to one of her pain medications. Because of this she lost the use of her legs and had to have physical therapy for a month. It was then that I decided to organize a major prayer campaign for Diane's recovery. I had prayed in the past, but I wanted thousands of prayers. Medical science was not helping. Everyone in the family contacted every Christian they knew and asked them to ask their churches to pray. I contacted the TGIF Group, every pastor, ministry leader, and friend that I knew. A plea was written for specific prayer in *The Christian Inmate News*. There is a possibility that as many as 100,000 prayers went up on her behalf, but certainly over 10,000. Since the beginning of the prayer project Diane's health has improved tenfold. She is now well on most days, and continues to improve. Her doctors are surprised at her recovery — they don't have an answer for what has changed. Prayer is what has affected Diane's health!

To give you an idea of the power of prayer, the disciples prayed for days. *Acts 1:12-14* Then Peter spoke for ten minutes *Acts 2:14-36* and 3,000 nonbelievers were saved. *Acts 2:41* "Until you know that life is war — you do not know what prayer is for!" (John Piper) A selfish request: If you decide that intercessory prayer is your ministry please pray for Core Ministries and me, Dave Ray.

You have a ministry! (Remember, the loving wounded-healer is one of the most effective caregivers.)

Heavenly Father, let my hurts and heartaches not happen in vain. Permit my experiences to teach me well so that I can be helpful to others in handling difficult circumstances and problems.
Author Unknown

Personal Perspective Questions

1. Do you ever see your need or the needs of others as a "doorway" or "opportunity" to ministry?
2. Can you identify areas where you have been wounded in your life?
3. Did you ever wonder why God has allowed your suffering? What reason does *Philippians 1:14* give?
4. From what pain, need, or distress have you been released or found comfort?
5. According to *2 Corinthians 1:4* what is your duty?
6. Are you a "wounded-healer?" — If yes, what must you do? *Matthew 10:8*
7. What are three ways you can use to find others with similar wounds? How can you help them?
8. Do you agree there is no hope for the world apart from the message of Christ? Then what should you do?
9. Are you considering being a mentor? Finding a mentor? Are you praying accordingly?

Group Discussion Questions

1. Do you see faith as "an action word?" In *James 1:22-27* what does it say about listening but not obeying?
2. What ministries are available through the local church?
3. How has God prepared the church to minister?
4. Where does the power to minister come from? *See Zechariah 4:1-7*
5. How important is prayer? *Acts 1:12-14, 2:41*
6. Is being a "prayer warrior" an excuse not to work at something else?
7. How has God made each believer "unique"?
8. What should we say when someone says, "I'm afraid!"? What Bible verse(s) would you use?
9. A large part of helping others is listening. What are good listening skills?
10. Identify three ground rules in helping people with their wounds.
11. True or false? Mentoring and prayer warrior are two ministries for which everybody is already prepared. Why or why not?
12. Is this the proper sequence — God 1st, family 2nd, Church 3rd? Why or why not?
13. According to *Acts 9:15* Christ gave Paul the goal of being a witness of the gospel of grace. Do you suppose this assignment also applies to us? Why? Why not?

YOU CAN MAKE A SIGNIFICANT DIFFERENCE FOR ETERNITY... YOU CAN DO IT NOW!

CHAPTER EIGHT

WORKING WITH CHURCH OR PARACHURCH?

Finding your niche for ministry. Working within your own church body is a wonderful place to minister.

The Bible clearly tells us to assemble with other believers. *Hebrews 10:25* Christians are to be active in their local assembly. This is where we have our opportunity to show the world that we are Christians by our love for other believers. Our local church provides a place for worship, instruction, and fellowship. It administers the sacraments, provides discipline, and prepares its members to reach out to the community. These activities all work to build up the believer for the work of service. As in the first century Church, the responsibilities remain the same — the leaders deal with spiritual issues within the body, and equip the lay people to do the work of ministry to one another and to the world. Church leaders help us clarify biblical text and doctrine. (We need to know what is right and wrong and when we are standing on firm biblical ground.) Because we have the New Testament and a thousand years of clarifying work of the Church fathers, we are much

better off than the church workers in the book of Acts. If we have a question and cannot get to an elder to help, we can refer to a study Bible or reference book.

It is important to be involved in our local church. One church I attended had over 75 written job descriptions for workers within the fellowship. You can research what opportunities your church offers. You have a ministry!

If there is no ministry for you in your local church then seek opportunities in the parachurch arena where there is plenty of need. While working through the local church is the most desirable way to have a ministry, it is not the only way. I went outside the local church to serve and the Lord caused it to be very effective. Most things that a parachurch organization does can be done on a small scale within the church. However, to reach the most people and to bring together the best resources to focus on an issue, the parachurch is often better suited. These efforts include, but are not limited to, urban homelessness, crisis pregnancy intervention, prison ministry, youth and youth-at-risk ministries, as well as college campus and large scale evangelism efforts.

You already know a little of my story and how I got involved in parachurch work. It did not stop there. In 1990 I felt led to start a new parachurch ministry called Core Ministries. Its purpose has been to strengthen, equip, and encourage staff and lay leaders as they go about the business of ministry. Over the years Core has done leadership training seminars, developed devotional and mentoring tools, and finally put together a prison ministry program that can be used by individuals, local churches, and parachurch organizations. This jail and prison ministry effort is my passion.

Study of the criminal justice system (CJS) has shown me that there is little done (especially by the system itself) to equip inmates to better cope once they get out of prison. Not enough is done to promote a successful transition to the outside and there are plenty of things that happen inside to make their successful transition harder. There are almost two million men, women, and juveniles incarcerated in the USA. Many people think that we should lock up the criminal and throw away the key. In our fear we demonize criminals and many of them begin to believe, as the public does, that there is no hope of rehabilitation for them. Of the two million people incarcerated in the USA today, 98 percent will eventually be released, and most will come out much worse than when they went in. So, if we succeed in getting those who are incarcerated to believe they are demons, then some day soon we are going to have almost two million demons living next to us. Wouldn't it be much better to have law-abiding Christians living next door?

Law-abiding Christians coming out of prison can happen! It already is happening. It is possible to significantly reduce the recidivism rate (the rate at which released ex-offenders return to crime and then prison). Success happens when a Christian inmate is given a Bible, and is put together with an equipped caring volunteer who helps the inmate network into a local church upon release. This is no pipe dream. Many government agencies are becoming interested in faith-based programs of rehabilitation because they are working when nothing else is. In Texas, the governor has invited the Christian Church into the prisons to do such a work and it has proven effective.

Other Parachurch Ministries:

If the criminal justice or rescue mission fields do not interest you, then there are many other part-time ministry fields to consider. They range from crisis pregnancy counselor to suicide prevention phone operator and many others in between. If your family does not suffer, there is no reason why you cannot work in both a church and parachurch ministry — I have done it for years.

Conflict between church and parachurch sometimes does occur. If it happens in your situation, don't let it throw you off balance.

I recently attended a meeting of a Christian coalition that is international and interdenominational in character. Most attendees' primary goal is to take Jesus to addicts and help them get sober and stay sober through their new-found faith. What a wonderful experience it was to be with 75 ministries from all over the world. Sadly though, while there I was also reminded of the tensions that can exist between church and parachurch organizations. While most attendees had wonderful relationships with their local churches, some parachurch leaders made public confessions about fostering resentment toward the organized church.

Maybe understanding both the need for parachurch organizations, and the tensions that can occur between church and parachurch will help to resolve them. There are over 30,000 denominations in the world plus tens of thousands of unaffiliated local churches. This diversity sometimes gets in the way of all churches working together. The parachurch was established to serve a need without considering doctrinal distinctives.

Parachurch organizations are specialized Christian Ministries. They were born of necessity to fill a need. Some do direct ministry; others support those in ministry through publishing, translation, or education.

Even though parachurch organizations can be doing a good work, there are some church leaders who believe that if the church isn't doing it, then it does not need to be done. Of course, both church and parachurch can and do vie for the dollars and talents of the same workers. Some parachurch leaders complain that the local church will not take in their new converts and disciple them. This is at times understandable when the converts are just out of prison, newly rehabilitated drug addicts, or street people. Churches have a hard time embracing people they don't understand or trust. Maybe even more so if they didn't actually bring them into the church themselves! Nobody wants his spouse and children sitting next to someone who could harm them. (This issue can be resolved by teaching the local church how to minister to those who have been down-and-out and are now redeemed.)

We don't let the fox guard the hen house, but we can let the fox in the hen house while chaperoned. Put another way, we don't have a known child molester teach children's Sunday school class or let them ever be alone with a child. (They also should not want to be put into that position.)

The key to the Christian life is balance. In this case we balance the needs of the one we are ministering to and the responsibility we have to our family and others in the church.

CAUTION: When ministering to dysfunctional people we have to keep clear in our mind the difference between <u>forgiveness</u> and the <u>consequences of sin</u>. God forgives us if we ask properly, but the consequences sometimes still remain with us. Both you and the person you are ministering to need to keep this in mind. You especially need to be above reproach in the specific sin area on which you are working. Both of you need to keep out of harm's way, for their sake, your sake, and the sake of others.

Personal Perspective Questions

1. How important is the local church to you? *Hebrews 10:24-25* — Notice the words "let us".
2. How do you show that the local church is important in your life?
3. What "passion" has God given you? Can it best be done in the church or a parachurch organization?
4. What good works are unique to your situation that can be done in your day-to-day life, that do not need to be done through the church or parachurch?
5. Take a moment to ask God what needs of others you have passed over this week that you could have filled?
6. Is there anyone you can think of who is down and out that could use an act of kindness to brighten their day? What are you waiting for?
7. How would you feel sitting next to an ex-offender? Why? How should you respond?
8. How do you think God wants us to treat ex-offenders?
9. How would you feel if your spouse or children were sitting next to an ex-offender? Why?
10. What does *1 Corinthians 13* teach about how to deal with one another?
11. How do you balance the command to forgive with the need to protect your loved ones?

Group Discussion Questions

1. What does the local church provide?
2. Why do we need leaders in the church?
3. Why is the local church "primary"?
4. What are the qualifications of pastors? elders? *1 Timothy 3:1-13, Titus 1:5-16*
5. What can a parachurch do that a local church cannot?
6. Should you neglect the local church for a parachurch?
7. What ministries are needed today in your community?
8. What can you do as a group to help these needs?
9. How many parachurch ministries and organizations can you think of?
10. Why do we have parachurch groups?
11. Should the local church and parachurch work together? Why or why not?
12. How should we welcome those who are different from us?
13. Does the world see the church as people who love or hate? A place of refuge or danger?
14. How should we be sensitive to the concerns of the church and parachurch when doing our ministries?
15. How does forgiveness and acceptance of these groups manifest itself in the church setting? Examples — alcoholics, drug addicts, mentally ill, homosexuals, and abusers. Can you add to this list?

YOU CAN MAKE A SIGNIFICANT DIFFERENCE FOR ETERNITY... YOU CAN DO IT NOW!

CHAPTER NINE

ORKING WITH OTHERS

We must be more interested in doing right (acting Christ-like) than being right (getting our way).

Christians cannot see either the God they worship or the enemy they fight. Is it any wonder there are well-meaning Christians who have differing opinions? Even the best intentioned Christians can get caught up in conflict with one another. Some of the most painful people to deal with are those who think they must prevail. (You know the type — they're right and you're wrong, or 'their way or the highway'. Everything must be a win-lose situation. They win and you lose.) These people want to bring their doctrinal distinctives into everything they do. Yet the Bible says that, *There are six things the LORD hates—no, seven things he detests... a person who sows discord among brothers. Proverbs 6:16-19*

When we hear people who are so sure of their theology, be reminded of a quote attributed to John Calvin. He said, "You can only believe 70 percent of what any theologian says. The problem is finding out which 30 percent not to believe." When we think about it, there are many areas of disagreement in human interpretation of the Bible. We can be sure God has only one meaning to a passage — one interpretation, but many applications. The problem is that mortal man thinks he knows exactly what that interpretation is even when there are respected Bible-believing theologians who believe otherwise.

Theologians who accept the Bible as God's Word agree on the major truths taught within it. However, scholars of equal intelligence, education, and intellectual honesty can and do disagree on many secondary issues. If God wanted the Bible to be crystal clear on every point, He could have easily accomplished that goal with a series of key verses. Clearly, He has not done that. Nevertheless, He wants us to have unity. Therefore, we should not allow the secondary issues to interfere with unity on a personal level.

Personal convictions can also get in the way of getting along with other believers. If the Bible says it is a sin, then it is a sin. The Bible also says that if you think it is a sin then it is a sin for you. But it is not necessarily one for others. These areas we call personal convictions. Saint Paul deals with this issue when he talks about eating meat sacrificed to idols. *1 Corinthians 8* We are not to elevate a personal conviction to the level of a Biblical command. Personal convictions are just that,

personal and should be avoided when working with others.

Sometimes we may have our mind set on a certain ministry. We are sure it's a needed ministry caring for others; and yet, we can't get the church to back it or other believers to get on board. We really believe God wants this ministry for us, but doors keep closing. At times like this, put the idea on hold for a year and then revisit it. Remember God is bigger than we are. He may be using others to tell us to find another work. A good rule is if you can't convince a majority of church leadership, it isn't a good idea at that time.

Also just because others agree that our ministry is a worthy one, we should not expect them to chip in and help. It may be that no one is interested in helping with our ministry. Others may not see what we see as worthy of their efforts. If we think about it, there are plenty of people involved in great ministries that we would not want to do ourselves, so why should we expect them to be involved in ours? Then again you might have the next Campus Crusade for Christ, World Vision, or Focus on the Family. However, to begin with, other's approval has to be enough! We need to remain faithful, and remember that God will provide help when He thinks we need it.

I get very excited about my jail, prison, and rescue mission ministry. God has given me that passion and I found out long ago that there are many other good causes for Christ that do not interest me as much as these. So, I concentrate on this ministry and don't get upset at others who do not see what I do as important. Christians are a body of individuals doing the total work of Christ — each doing something a little different. *1 Corinthians 12:12-31* That's okay, and we are to encourage others to get involved, but don't feel guilty if you do not help in every need there is. Expect God to call someone else to work on that need.

We must be more interested in doing right (acting Christ-like) than being right (getting our way). Don't be blown away with dissension in the church. Remember what is said about churches with active members, "Where there is body activity there is bound to be some body odor — it's normal."

The Need for Cooperation:

When I began my duties on the Board of Directors at a parachurch ministry, I was ignorant of the workings of the organization. I asked the chairman if it was okay if I attended the weekly staff meetings as an observer with no official board authority. I promised that I would not speak for the board or even give opinions of the board. The chairman thought this was a great idea, so my education began. After a few months of attending these meetings, many things became apparent to my businessman's eye. I felt it was time to start implementing changes.

When I started discussions at the board level about how they should begin, they would talk and talk, yet very little was getting done. They got nowhere because I was trying to sell my solutions. It became apparent that my effort got them away from the real work at hand. Since they were getting nowhere in accomplishing the changes they all felt were needed to maximize the ministry, I decided it was time to change my methods.

I got away from discussing theory and "what ifs" and instead presented written plans and programs I believed would make for a more efficient and effective management. My goal was to get them started, and then let the group rework my plan/program to suit themselves. This was just what they did. They would begin with a section, and then the board would modify it. I would agree to make the changes. They would then move on until all the questions were asked and suggestions handled. Once the changes were all approved they would have a new policy, plan, or procedure ready to implement. It was now theirs, not mine. I had to do a lot of work in developing the original plan, but after the others modified it, we had a great plan. The others used their professional skills and empirical knowledge gained from years of working on the board to improve my basic plan. The new plan was much better than any one of them could have created alone, and they all had ownership of it when it was finished. A President Reagan quote fits here; "It's amazing what you can accomplish if you don't care who gets the credit."

If I had been stubborn and tried to push across my plan it never would have worked. My job was to help the others get started, so that they could use their wisdom and knowledge to perfect the plan. My responsibility was to get a plan approved. It did not have to be my plan. I was more interested in doing right than being right — put another way, I put the needs of others ahead of my opinion. I feel good about the accomplishments the ministry made while I was part of its leadership, and the progress it continues to make building on the work we did years ago. You may say, "How does this apply to me in my ministry endeavor?" If you keep your eyes on the goal and not the methods, you will be able to compromise methods and gain support.

> ## Methods are many,
> ## Principles are few.
> ## Principles never change,
> ## Methods often do.

There are normally many right ways to do a job, and we must keep that in mind when we work with others. Their right way may be just as appropriate as our right way. Think about the goal more than the methods! Give methods the leeway, not the goal. On the other hand, principles must not be compromised.

If you are getting a lot of resistance as you work within a group, talk to your pastor to be sure you are on firm theological ground. We also want to be sure that the issue is one of principle and not method. If it is a method issue, be willing to submit — it is good for your character. If it is a principle issue, resist — it is also good for your character.

The work of caregiving is the goal—The goal should not be that things are done only your way. You have a ministry!

Personal Perspective Questions

1. What was Paul's response to division in the Corinthian Church? *1 Corinthians 1:10*
2. What does Paul say can be one reason for division? *1 Corinthians 11:18-19*
3. According to *Proverbs 6:16-19*, what does God hate?
4. Why is it more important for us to act like Christ than to get our way?
5. Are you the cause of any "body odor" in your church?
6. Who is the greatest in the Kingdom of God? *Matthew 18:1-5*
7. What is better: that we get the credit/glory or God gets the glory? Why?
8. How should we look at others? *Philippians 2:3* Look at our leaders? *1 Thessalonians 5:12-13*
9. Should we be upset if someone changes or modifies our plan? Why or why not.

Group Discussion Questions

1. Why are there divisions in the church?
2. For what did Jesus pray? *John 17:11* How does this apply to your church?
3. What does *Philippians 2:1-4* teach? *Psalm 133:1?*
4. When should we stop pursuing a ministry we feel is needed when the rest of the church does not feel it is needed?
5. How should we deal with differing opinions?
6. How does *1 Corinthians 12:12-31* help us decide the worth of a ministry?
7. How does *1 Peter 3:15-16* apply to this chapter?
8. When can we leave the theological battles to the theologians, and do good works with other Christians on a personal level?
9. In *Romans chapter 14* what responsibilities do the more mature believers have when dealing with differences of opinion in the church?
10. What should our goal be when working with a group? Why?
11. How can "my plan" be changed to "our plan" without hurting anyone's feelings?
12. What does it mean to "put the needs of others ahead of my opinions"?
13. Why are principles more important than methods?
14. How many ways are there to accomplish a goal?

YOU CAN MAKE A SIGNIFICANT DIFFERENCE FOR ETERNITY... YOU CAN DO IT NOW!

THE FOOT OF THE CROSS

CHAPTER TEN

For the sake of the work, Christians need to come together at the foot of the cross and do what God clearly calls them to do.

Although I am a layman, I recognize how important denominational issues are. All we need is a short course in Church history to see that many thousands have given their very lives for these distinctives. History shows that the Church does not come together, but rather starts together, then separates into factions. These divisions are often important in moving the church forward and in understanding God's purposes for His people. Sometimes these factions divide us into enemy camps. At the same time the New Testament is filled with commands for Christians to love one another. Yet when we read today's newspapers, "They will know we are Christians by our love" seems to have become, "They will know we are Christians by our back-biting or angry divisions." It's time for a change.

One of the main roles of the Church in the 21st century is to be unified against the forces of evil. The need for this unity is becoming acute. We have so much work to do for the poor and the lost that we do not have the time to waste disagreeing with each other. I have spent my Christian career trying to find a common ground, so I can work with others at doing the work clearly mandated in scripture. It is time for Christians to get together and find that common piece of ground, one that all Christians can stand on in unity without compromising denominational distinctives. Then, we can get on with the work and have the blessings of our church leaders.

Many have heard church leaders say that in the kingdom unity is not sameness, but oneness. This is a valid truth. If the Church is going to be effective in meeting *Matthew 25,* we are going to have to find "common kingdom ground" where unity of purpose, sameness of heart, and oneness of vision eliminate denominational distinctives. Common vision brings about unity. When there is a common work that all are engaged in, there is less conflict. An observation of successful group endeavors is that all members have a spirit of cooperation and desire to do the right thing. In ministry, this happens when individual believers come together at the foot of Christ's cross. A good example of this kind of unity was the *Promise Keepers Stand-in-the-Gap* assembly in Washington in 1997. (See *John 17:20-21* unity among the Godhead -- unity in the body of Christ.)

To get to the foot of the cross it is important for us to travel upstream to where all denominations spiritually originated. The foot of the cross is the level ground, the plateau where there are no doctrinal distinctives. It is in fact the highest spiritual ground in the kingdom. The foot is a place where all believers are equal, the preacher and the pauper, the prostitute and plumber, the president and Pope. For the sake of the work, Christians need to come together at the foot of the cross and do what God clearly calls them to do. Let's do our ministry outside areas of controversy. What would this look like?

There is not one parent that does not want his or her children to get along with each other. Would God be any different? Can you in your wildest imagination visualize us acting in heaven the way we act here? The challenge is to put our doctrinal distinctives aside, along with our need to be right. We need to do the right thing - do the things we would do if we stood at the foot of the cross and Christ was watching. He is, you know. Where confession is needed, let us confess. Where forgiveness is needed, let us forgive. Where tolerance is needed, let us tolerate. Above all, let's have patience with each other, but no patience about fighting Satan.

Bobb Biehl, Christian organizational consultant and author, says that a "tennis pastor" will not be happy in a "bowling church". Likewise I do not think a "tennis member" will be happy in a "bowling church" either. The truth is that people pick their local fellowship not only on doctrinal issues alone, but also on social, vocational, cultural, and ethnic issues. That's okay! However, the work of the capital "C" Church (Body of Christ) attempted outside the local assembly should be accomplished in an atmosphere where we only bring Foot-Of-The-Cross issues to the table. We need to leave our tennis racquets and bowling balls behind. We have to agree that we are all part of the Body of Christ — having duties to both our local fellowship and to the whole kingdom of God. When it is a whole kingdom issue we must put our local fellowship issues aside and work for the larger purpose of being a witness for Christ to the nations. We need to see the big picture, not just a portion of it.

The first big step is to mobilize the laity to work on the "caregiving" issues mentioned in *Matthew 25:31-46*. We can agree on these issues. They all fit at the foot of the cross.

They include:

- Feeding the hungry
- Providing drink for the thirsty
- Being hospitable to strangers
- Clothing the naked
- Visiting the sick
- Visiting the prisoners

Note: With each work we are telling of Christian Salvation

We have heard "you must agree to disagree agreeably". For the sakes of the least and the lost, "you must agree to agree"— period. Below are listed ten items that all Christians could agree upon without compromising denominational distinctives. These all fit at the foot of the cross.

1. The Bible is the Word of God.
   2 Timothy 3:16-17; Proverbs 30:5-6

2. There is one God who exists in three Persons: Father, Son, and Holy Spirit.
   Matthew 28:19; John 14:10-11,20

3. Jesus is both man and God. He was born of a virgin and led a sinless life. He performed miracles. He died on the cross for our sins. He rose from the dead. He has gone to be with the Father. He will return in power and glory someday. *Colossians 1:15-23; Matthew 1:25; 2 Corinthians 5:21; Matthew 11:20; Hebrews 12:2;: 1 Thessalonians 4:13-18*

4. The Holy Spirit lives in Christians, enabling them to live a Godly life.
   Romans 8; Galatians 5:16

5. There will be a resurrection of both the saved and the lost; the saved to Heaven and the lost to Hell.
   Matthew 25:31-46, Acts 24:15

6. There must be spiritual unity of believers in our Lord Jesus Christ.
   1 Corinthians 12:21-31

7. Christians are called to love one another. *John 13:34*

8. We are called to feed the poor, clothe the naked, and visit the prisoners.
   Matthew 25:31-46

9. The believer's real enemy is Satan and his hordes. *Ephesians 6:12*

10. We must keep an eternal view of life.
    Revelation 20:11, 2 Corinthians 5:10

What we need is a way for us all to agree on certain works and then do them — whether through the church, the parachurch or both. The job is big enough for us all. Every individual Christian, whether in a local church, denomination or parachurch, is part of the Body of Christ. If we could put energy into finding ways for all to work together, the problem would be solved. We all need to work our ministry.

I ran across a chart in 1987 that has helped me decide what issues really matter to me. When I began working in trans-denominational parachurch activities it helped me to decide what things were best to avoid while working with people from other Christian churches. I tried to keep in mind "In essentials unity, in nonessentials liberality, and in all things charity." I call the chart "The Circle of Tolerance". If your ministry takes you where you work with people from other churches, use the chart to help you identify the areas you should be able to tolerate and the ones you won't. (For examples see question 16 in the "Group Discussion Questions" at the end of this chapter.)

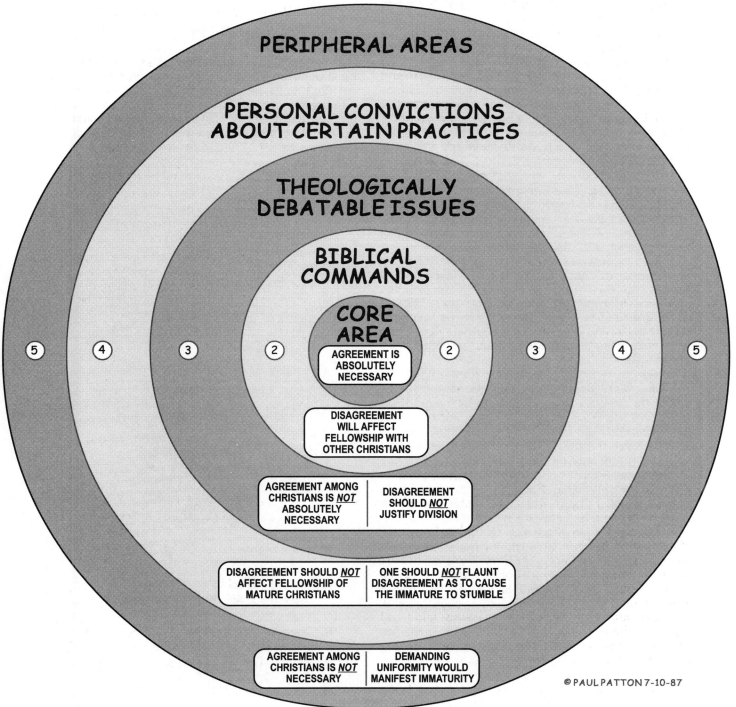

PERIPHERAL AREAS

PERSONAL CONVICTIONS ABOUT CERTAIN PRACTICES

THEOLOGICALLY DEBATABLE ISSUES

BIBLICAL COMMANDS

CORE AREA

AGREEMENT IS ABSOLUTELY NECESSARY

DISAGREEMENT WILL AFFECT FELLOWSHIP WITH OTHER CHRISTIANS

AGREEMENT AMONG CHRISTIANS IS _NOT_ ABSOLUTELY NECESSARY | DISAGREEMENT SHOULD _NOT_ JUSTIFY DIVISION

DISAGREEMENT SHOULD _NOT_ AFFECT FELLOWSHIP OF MATURE CHRISTIANS | ONE SHOULD _NOT_ FLAUNT DISAGREEMENT AS TO CAUSE THE IMMATURE TO STUMBLE

AGREEMENT AMONG CHRISTIANS IS _NOT_ NECESSARY | DEMANDING UNIFORMITY WOULD MANIFEST IMMATURITY

5 4 3 2 2 3 4 5

© PAUL PATTON 7-10-87

YOUR MINISTRY... anything you do to strengthen others!

The bulls-eye of "The Circle of Tolerance" chart are those "Foot Of The Cross" issues mentioned earlier in this chapter. Many have found that when we focus on the ministry there is no problem working with other Christians.

If we are going to serve God, we must be aware of Satan. He does not want us to succeed in ministry. He is the father of lies *John 8:44*; he hides the truth of the gospel *Matthew 13:19*; he is like a roaring lion, seeking to destroy us. *1 Peter 5:8* The Bible says he can disguise himself like an angel of light or purity. *2 Corinthians 11:14* He used to be the most beautiful of angels. *Ezekiel 28:11-15* He was even called "the son of the dawn" and "the morning star" until he decided he wanted the power and the worship due to God and God alone. *Isaiah 14:12-15* Satan and his demons will go to great lengths to limit our effectiveness. They may cause divisions in our church. They may seek to bring conflict between church and parachurch organizations. They may attack our families, finances, or our faith. Satan is not someone to be discounted. We need to be aware of him and his actions.

Paul teaches us just who our enemies really are — *For we are not fighting against people made of flesh and blood, but against the evil rulers and authorities of the unseen world, against those mighty powers of darkness who rule this world, and against wicked spirits in the heavenly realms. Ephesians 6:12* We need to be aware of these spiritual forces and learn how they work in the world today so we will be ready to stand against them. Study scripture first to see how Christ and His followers battled evil. *Matthew 4:1-11; Acts 4:19-20* Then recognize what the dangers are so you can avoid them. Remember, *Be careful! Watch out for attacks from the Devil, your great enemy. He prowls around like a roaring lion, looking for some victim to devour. Take a firm stand against him, and be strong in your faith. Remember that Christians all over the world are going through the same kind of suffering you are. 1 Peter 5:8-9*

Being aware of his desire to defeat us enables us to act wisely. Understand that Satan and his demons sneak into your life when you let your guard down or leave a door open to your mind or heart. For instance, if we are angry and do not forgive, we can give the devil a foothold, the place where he can work evil into our life. *Ephesians 4:27* Or if we sin and do not repent, he has room to move in and encourage us further in this area. Whenever Satan comes against us, we do have weapons to stand against him. We need to remember to use them. Jesus said He has given you the authority you need to overcome the enemy's power. *Luke 10:19* Satan is real; he is powerful; and he is very tricky but we are protected if we put on the armor God has for us. *Use every piece of God's armor to resist the enemy in the time of evil, so that after the battle you will still be standing firm. Stand your ground, putting on the sturdy belt of truth and the body armor of God's righteousness. For shoes, put on the peace that comes from the Good News, so that you will be fully prepared. In every battle you will need faith as your shield to stop the fiery arrows aimed at you by Satan. Put on salvation as your helmet, and take the sword of the Spirit, which is the word of God. Pray at all times and on every occasion in the power of the Holy Spirit. Stay alert and be persistent in your prayers for all Christians everywhere. Ephesians 6:13-18*

The Bible tells us that the Christian life is a battle. Like all soldiers, Christians have a commander and weapons to fight the enemy. The best part about this war is that victory is sure. All Christians can count on God supplying them the grace to endure. Now with that said, understand that not every problem is Satan's fault. He is the tempter but he cannot make us do anything. We choose by the evil nature that lives in us. *James 1:14-15*

Living by the Spirit's Power

So I advise you to live according to your new life in the Holy Spirit. Then you won't be doing what your sinful nature craves. The old sinful nature loves to do evil, which is just opposite from what the Holy Spirit wants. And the Spirit gives us desires that are opposite from what the sinful nature desires. These two forces are constantly fighting each other, and your choices are never free from this conflict. But when you are directed by the Holy Spirit, you are no longer subject to the law. Galatians 5:16-18

Keep in mind that Satan may not be in our mess at all. We could be doing such a good job ourselves thwarting our own efforts that Satan has the time to work on someone else.

Personal Perspective Questions

1. According to *Ephesians 6:10-20* what seven things have been given to us so we may stand against the Devil and his hordes?
2. Using the verses in the beginning of this chapter, describe the Devil.
3. How did Jesus answer the Devil? *Matthew 4:1-11*
4. When the Devil tempts you, what do you say?
5. Do you believe Satan is real, evil, powerful and our mortal enemy?
6. Does Satan have a foothold in your life? Do you believe Satan is keeping you from a ministry? What should you do?
7. How can we love those who are in a different denomination?
8. What is the key mark of a Christian? *1 Corinthians 13:13*

Group Discussion Questions

1. How can we encourage one another to stand against the Devil? *Ephesians 6:10-20* especially 19-20
2. How does *1 Corinthians 10:13* and *I Peter 5:8-9* give us encouragement?
3. How can we be a "wounded-healer" to one who has yielded to the attack of Satan?
4. How does *1 Peter 3:13-14* apply to fear while doing works of ministry?
5. Martin Luther said our enemies are the world, the flesh and the Devil. God has supplied us with His grace to stand against these foes. The means of this grace are Bible reading, Prayer, Worship, Fellowship, and Service. This author thinks that the Christian's fourth enemy is willful neglect of these graces. In what ways can we make better use of these means-of-grace in strengthening our walk with Christ?
6. This book deals with Service but we should be concerned with all five means of grace. How can we have a balanced approach in dealing with our three biggest enemies?
7. Satan originally wanted to be God but failed. Because he could not dethrone God, he opposes Him by attacking His followers. *1 Peter 5:8* Satan strikes at God by tempting us to sin. How is God glorified by our victory over a specific sin? By us enduring suffering? What verses come to mind?
8. How will you act with other believers in heaven? Should we try to act that way now?
9. Is it possible to keep our distinctives and still work with other Christians? How?
10. In what ways can we work for our local church and not ignore the whole kingdom of God?
11. Is it necessary to solve all theological differences before we can work together?
12. What are the points of doctrine that you can agree on? Why are these crucial?
13. Is doctrine important? *I Timothy 4:12-15*
14. Why is working with someone from another church sometimes different than working with someone from our own church?
15. Are there any doctrinal distinctives that should divide us into enemy camps?
16. In what ring of the "circle of tolerance" would you place the following potentially divisive issues? Murder, suicide, playing baseball on Sunday, the existence of God, dancing, co-ed volleyball, dating non-Christians, marrying non-Christians, speaking in tongues, the deity of Jesus, adultery, swim suit apparel, pornography, one's political position, smoking cigarettes, smoking marijuana, getting drunk, drinking alcoholic beverages, resurrection of Jesus, watching TV, post- or pre-tribulation position, authority of scripture, listening to rock music, infant baptism, abortion, slavery, worship on Saturday, women leaders in the church, creation, can we lose our salvation?, divorce, racism, the tri-unity of God, virgin birth of Jesus, pacifism, the existence of hell.
17. Why do some Christians have a way of emphasizing the 10 percent that separates them instead of the 90 percent that unites them?

YOU CAN MAKE A SIGNIFICANT DIFFERENCE FOR ETERNITY...
YOU CAN DO IT NOW!

STANDING ON SOLID THEOLOGICAL GROUND

The Church must be protected from heresy and sometimes for the sake of the health of a fellowship, we will need to be a black sheep - one who stands alone when it is the right thing to do.

The beginning of this book talked about my experience as a new believer, and how the local church at first did not apply my talents to the best use. This book has also stated that a brand new believer can be put to work almost immediately. Studies show the sooner the better. Most new believers want to serve but if we wait until they are spiritually trained, they may lose that desire. *1 Peter 4:10-11* and *Ephesians 4:1-13* are clear in saying that each and every believer has a ministry. The key is to identify what that ministry is.

The spiritual work of the early church was done by the Apostles and the everyday work by the laity. *Acts 6:1-6* The same ratio (spiritual leaders to laity) is needed in the local church today. Relatively few spiritual leaders (prophets, evangelists, apostles, and pastor-teachers) are needed compared to the number of lay men and women needed to do the work in the church. We may conclude that this is playing down the leader's work and playing up the believer's individual ministry. That is not what I want to communicate. What I want to make abundantly clear is that the local church must be protected from heresy. Most of us are not equipped to be spiritual leaders, and it takes years to gain the knowledge needed to be an effective spiritual leader.

In an earlier chapter I told the story about my early work on the board of a parachurch because my local church did not recognize my management and organizational abilities. That work at the parachurch had the complete support of my pastor. Later with the church leadership's blessings, I started a very successful singles' ministry in the church. I also led a land acquisition campaign where the congregation's unanimous vote was to purchase six acres of land.

I reported to the pastor or the board and was their servant. I do not believe that I should have been considered for an official church leadership position because I was not trained enough in theology to have met the biblical requirements for such leadership.

My vocational background is as an instrumentation engineer and a businessman. Engineering at times is very technical and hard to understand. I had always believed that engineering

and the sciences were by far the hardest things to master. After just a few months of Bible and theological study, I changed my mind. I now believe that the most technical and difficult of human endeavors is the study of theology. The theologians have their own very technical vocabulary — more technical than engineering. We owe our understanding as to what God's Word means to the theologians and their church councils throughout history.

We need theologians who support the teachings of the church fathers. We need to surrender to the spiritual authority of our local church. Few are called, qualified, and dedicated enough to be spiritual leaders. We need to thank God every day for our spiritual leaders. Strong-willed powerful people can come into a church and think just because they manage 50 or 100 people, or millions of dollars that they are qualified to be church leaders. Their backgrounds shouldn't keep them from taking special assignments in the local church/ministry where their talents can help the organization become a better steward of God's resources. However, the key is that they surrender to serve Jesus. The sign of that surrender is their willingness to submit to the spiritual authorities of their local church.

The first way to protect from heresy is to read what the Bible has to say, then ask ourselves and others "what did the church fathers say about this?" Be very wary of new interpretations. Let scripture interpret scripture. The Bible says sin abounds. Heresy has to be one of the worst sins.

Let's pray for and support our spiritual leaders, and if you think you have found a "new" interpretation you probably have not. The serpent told Eve she would be as God. Today's New Age movement says the same. Harry Truman said, "The only thing new in life is the history you do not know." It follows that the only new heresy is the church history you do not know.

It is understandable for our church leaders to <u>want</u> consensus. When they say they <u>need</u> consensus watch out! All Satan would have to do is get to one person in order to have control over the whole body.

We are called to be peacemakers, not wimps. *Matthew 5:9, Romans 12:18* This can be explained by using Jesus' commands when He sent out the disciples. The first time He sent them He said, *"Don't even take along a walking stick," he instructed them, "nor a traveler's bag, nor food, nor money. Not even an extra coat." Luke 9:3* At a later time, *Then Jesus asked them, "When I sent you to preach the Good News and you did not have money, a traveler's bag, or extra clothing, did you lack anything?" "No," they replied. "But now" he said, "take your money and a traveler's bag. And if you don't have a sword, sell your clothes and buy one!" Luke 22: 35-36* The first time He said get rid of your sword. The second time He said, "sell your coat if necessary, but take a sword." In other words there are times to seek peace—do it first. But there are also times to fight. Remember the limerick?

> Methods are many,
> Principles are few.
> Principles never change,
> Methods often do.

If you are having difficulty with conflict, seek counsel and ask for scripture references so you can decide if you are talking about methods or principles. Then answer the question, "Will this really have any eternal consequences?" If how we handle the issue in question does have eternal consequences, the hard decision becomes — is this an issue in which we need to use the sword? Is it an issue that requires confrontation and a firm stand?

God hates dissension in the brotherhood. *Proverbs 6:19* There is no question about that. However, there is a question we need to ask: Are we causing dissension or just rooting out the dissenter? There are too many times when a church member has not been properly confronted and disciplined. Sometimes this neglect has led to a church split, or the destruction of that fellowship's witness in the community. Sometimes for the sake of the health of a fellowship, we will need to be a black sheep —one who stands alone when it is the right thing to do.

People attend church and get involved in ministry for many different reasons. Most surveys show that only a little more than half of the people who go to church would agree with the ten basic tenets of faith listed in chapter ten, "The Foot Of The Cross." It may be because they have not studied the issues or just don't understand their importance. Yet, we are part of the family of God and the local church is our family home. We already know that every family is weird in one way or another. Just the same as there is no perfect family, there is no perfect church/ministry family.

In the world you have faultfinders and those that encourage, fighters and peace makers, positive thinkers and the negative thinkers, those who are responsible and those who are victims, rich and poor, smart and not-so-smart, complainers and those who suffer quietly, the selfish and the generous, givers and takers, helpers and those that hinder, legalists and the more tolerant, people with handicaps and people without handicaps, builders and those that tear down, the sympathetic and the harsh. Don't be surprised when some of these type people make it into your church. In short, all kinds of people make up the Church.

Even so we are called to love one another, yet sometimes loving each other is a very difficult thing. When I am having difficulty with a brother or sister, my mind takes me to a scene in the movie ET. The main character is an extra terrestrial being who had a heart light that lit up when he was feeling love. Wouldn't it be wonderful if all Christians had a heart light? When we first believe in God a small light would show through our clothes for all to see. Then as we grow in our faith the light gets brighter and brighter. The light might even dim or flash when our old nature is taking over — much like Pinocchio's nose growing when he lied. It would be so much easier to read people!

We don't always know if someone we are in fellowship with is acting in love. That is why it's important not to demand consensus, rewards, or accolades here and now. Instead, dream and hope for that phrase, "Well done my good and faithful servant." It is not realistic to expect 100% support from others in the family of God. It is nice to have others agree with what we are doing, but remember we are doing our ministry to please God by obeying His command. *Ephesians 4:11-13* As we serve the Lord, we will encounter both physical and spiritual relatives who will not understand what we are doing. They may even put roadblocks in our path. Do not react negatively to these individuals. Instead, try to treat them politely and go about your business. God didn't supply us with heart lights, but we can make others' hearts light up by following our ministry.

Don't be discouraged by the nay-sayers. Don't even try to change them with words. Pour burning coals on their heads by your unselfish actions for the Lord. *Proverbs 25:21-22; Romans 12:19-21* Just get started and get the job done!

Personal Perspective Questions

1. Why is it important to study the Bible? *II Timothy 2:15*
2. In *Ephesians 4:11-16* what is the role of our church leaders and what is our responsibility?
3. What is the key to your service?
4. How do you protect your own beliefs from heresy? *1 Timothy 3:16-17*
5. Did Paul love Peter in *Galatians 2:1-21 (verse 11)*
6. How are we to correct another Christian? *Ephesians 4:15*
7. Is there ever a time for harshness? *Romans 12:19-21, I Timothy 1:20*
8. When should we stop seeking reconciliation and instead fight? Read all of *Jude*
9. We should always seek peace but sometimes we have to go to war to have true peace. Will we always be able to be at peace with others? *Romans 12:18*
10. After you see something that needs to be done, what do you need before you do that good deed?

Group Discussion Questions

1. According to *Acts 6:4*, what were the leaders to do?
2. Do you agree the leader's role is to protect and lead the flock? Why or Why not? *Hebrews 13:7,17; 1 Peter 5:1-3*
3. What is the laity's role?
4. How are the leaders and lay people to work together?
5. How does ignoring history hurt the church?
6. How often should we ask ourselves, "Will this have any eternal consequences?"
7. Do most divisions come from opinions or rooting out error?
8. What did Jesus teach in *Matthew 18:15-20?* Give an example of how this could be used in the Church today.
9. In *Acts 20:29-30* Jesus tells us that we will encounter false teachers in the churches. How do we stand up against this evil?
10. What is the caution in *Jude 23?*
11. What significance is there in *James 5:19-20?*
12. Since it is not realistic to expect 100% support for your ministry from others, what are some positive godly ways we can handle road blocks that others set up?
13. The oneness of all believers is that we are one in Body, Spirit, Hope, Lord, Faith, Baptism, and God. *Ephesians 4:4-6* Therefore when believers have unity of spirit, petty differences should never dissolve that unity. What issues have we allowed to cause dissension with other believers?

YOU CAN MAKE A SIGNIFICANT DIFFERENCE FOR ETERNITY... YOU CAN DO IT NOW!

DO NOT BE DISCOURAGED

What if the results we see aren't what we hoped for?

The simple answer is that we must remember that our work for God is never wasted. *1 Corinthians 15:58* As good stewards we are called to be faithful, not successful. *1 Corinthians 4:1-2*

However, it is nice to see the results of our work, and eventually we will. But it will sometimes have to wait until we hear, *"Well done, my good and faithful servant."* *Matthew 25:21*

Years ago when I gave some advice to a friend, the friend said, "Just who's milking this cow"? He implied it was his job, so he was doing it his way. Well, when it comes to works for the Lord, "He is milking the cow," so the results are likewise His.

I like it when I hear about how my ministry is helping people. Apparently God knew that I would be easily discouraged, so in His grace He sends me encouragement almost daily. On the other hand He also allows me to hear from the naysayers on a regular basis. I have come to see some of these attacks as a compliment, because if I weren't causing any harm to the cause of Satan, Satan would just leave me alone. So I see the attacks as a sign of being on the right track, and I attempt to stay there unless someone proves to me that it is unbiblical. Because there is so much discouragement in Christian service, I have, as one of my personal ministries, attempted to build up all Christian efforts — unless they are against the teaching of Scripture.

If by now you have not decided on a personal ministry why not consider a ministry of encouragement for those who are trying to do God's will by taking Christ's love and grace to the hurting? On the other hand, if you have decided to have a ministry of keeping everyone on the straight and narrow and to criticize and show all possible faults — do everyone a favor and don't. Many have already taken that job. They must feel they have the gift of criticism which is <u>not</u> a spiritual gift!

We do our good works as an act of gratitude to God for His saving grace. He knows our hearts, and the satisfaction of doing His will just has to be enough. In chapter ten I talked about how Satan wants to discourage us. We also must keep our mind straight so that our own thoughts of success do not discourage us. We must pray always to keep an eternal perspective on what we do and how we act.

The Mr. Jenner's Story told by Josh McDowell should help when you feel discouraged in ministry:

Mr. Jenner's Story

Dr. Francis Dixon is a well-known pastor in England. One night in church he asked a man named Peter to share his testimony. Peter got up and said, "This is how I was saved. I was in the Royal Navy; I was walking down George Street in Sydney, Australia and out of nowhere stepped a little old gray-haired man and he said to me, 'Excuse me, sir, but could I ask you a question? I hope that it won't offend you, but if you were to die today, where would you spend eternity? The Bible says that it will either be in Heaven or it will be in Hell. Would you think about that, please? Thank you, God bless you, and Toodle-oo!' Then the man left. I had never been confronted with that question — I couldn't get it out of my mind; I got back to London, I sought out a pastor, and I became a Christian."

Several weeks later they had a revival in the church and Noel, one of the visiting revival team, shared his testimony, "This is how I came to know Christ. I was in the Royal Navy and I was walking down George Street in Sydney, Australia and out of nowhere stepped a little old gray-haired man, He said to me, 'Excuse me, sir, but could I ask you a question? I hope that it won't offend you, but if you were to die today, where would you spend eternity? The Bible says that it will either be in Heaven or it will be in Hell. Would you think about that, please? Thank you, God bless you, and Toodle-oo!' What he said bothered me and later, I sought out a Christian and I was converted to Christ."

Several months after that Dr. Dixon was in the city of Adelaide in eastern Australia and he thought that he would share the testimony of Peter and Noel. A man in the congregation jumped up waving his hands and said, "Well, I'm another — the same thing happened to me. I couldn't get what he said out of my mind and I became a follower of Jesus."

Dr. Dixon went to western Australia for a revival meeting and shared this story and afterwards a deacon of the church came to him and said, "Dr. Dixon I'm another, I'd never been asked that question and later I prayed to receive Christ."

Pastor Dixon went home to his church in England and shared about Peter and Noel and the man in Adelaide and the deacon from the western part of Australia. When he finished, a young lady came up to him and said, "Pastor Dixon, I'm another, this man said the same thing to me and later I became a believer."

Several weeks after that, Dr. Dixon was attending a conference in northern England where he shared this growing story. Afterwards, a man came up to him and said, "Dr. Dixon, well, I'm another, several days after hearing the little man's question, I made Jesus my Lord and Savior."

A year later Dr. Dixon went on a world tour and one of the stops was India. He was at a missionary conference and spoke on the topic of personal evangelism. Dr. Dixon thought, "What a perfect illustration!" He went through the story and afterwards a missionary came up to him and said, "Dr. Dixon, I'm another, it happened the same way for me and I trusted Christ later."

After India he went to Jamaica. He was meeting with a group of pastors there he shared this story with them. A pastor came up afterwards and said, "Excuse me, Dr. Dixon, I'm another, the exact same thing happened to me and later, I was converted and went on to seminary."

Well, do I need to tell you where Dr. Dixon went? He went to Sydney, Australia, He sought out a Christian friend of his and told the story and asked if he knew a little gray-haired man on George Street? "Oh, yes! Everybody knows him. That's Mr. Jenner. He did that for twenty-three years! But he's very old now and he's in the hospital confined to his bed."

Dr. Dixon asked his friend to take him to Mr. Jenner. They went to the hospital and Dr. Dixon introduced himself and as he was giving specifics of each story Mr. Jenner began to weep. And he wept and he wept. Dr. Dixon finally asked, "What's wrong?" And Mr. Jenner said, "Sir, this is the first time in my life that I've ever known of anyone coming to know Christ through my witness."

A footnote by Josh McDowell:

In 1993 while speaking at a conference on evangelism in Orlando, Florida I shared the above story about Mr. Jenner and at the end of my talk a woman rushed to the front and blurted out, "I'm another… I was visiting friends in Australia when one evening I was walking down George Street and that little old man spoke to me…It happened to be that I was already a believer but his love and persistence so impacted me that I began to share my faith with others."

Then in 1994 a man, who had heard me in Orlando, approached me at the Atlanta, Georgia airport and said he was another. However, it was Peter, the first man named above that led him to Christ."

WOW! What a marvelous story.

I have heard Josh tell this story three times and I have gotten choked up every time I heard it. From a street corner in Sydney, Australia God used Mr. Jenner to affect lives for eternity in Eastern Australia, Western Australia, Northern England, Southern England, India and Jamaica — and those are only the ones we know about. When you get discouraged think about Mr. Jenner — I do!

An important comment: Mr. Jenner's story reminds me that I would be remiss if somewhere in this book I didn't say that the most important caregiving ministry is to care enough to share the Gospel. Always remember that caregiving works are in themselves life-style evangelism — one of the very best forms of evangelism. (Some people do not know how to share their faith so I have enclosed a copy of *the God's Original Plan* method of sharing your faith. See Appendix B)

Personal Perspective Questions

1. Is knowing you are trying your best to please God enough for you? Enough for Him?

2. Have you taken God at His word and do you know that your sins are forgiven? Do you have any sin that you have not confessed? Ask for forgiveness now!

3. Have you asked, "Am I an encourager?" Why or why not? How can your encouragement of others in their ministry endeavors change the life span of their ministry?

4. Are you aware that each good work you do is an end in itself and you have done your job? What God does beyond that is up to Him. He will accomplish His purposes through His Word. *Isaiah 55:11* Do you struggle with this?

5. Is there anyone you know who is not appreciated enough for their works of ministry? Why? How can you encourage them?

6. Would you rather have rewards here and now or hold off until Heaven? How about a little bit of each? Is there one right answer? (See questions at end of Chapter 6 "The Reward Paradox.")

7. Knowing that things take longer than expected, what promises do you have from scripture to hang on to when discouraged? Can you use these scriptures to also encourage others in their ministry?

Group Discussion Questions

1. Does it matter at all, from an eternal perspective, if we have a ministry on earth? Why? Why not?

2. Why do you suppose that God mostly does not reveal all of the effects of each ministry?

3. Do we have to encourage and support any and all organizations that use as part of their name the words Christ, Christian, Church, or Bible?

4. If you had been Mr. Jenner would you have continued witnessing without knowing the results? Is it possible that you have given up a viable ministry because of not knowing whether you were making a difference?

5. Many are busy in their own ministries. Why is it okay for others to agree that your cause is a good one yet not support it with their time or money?

YOU CAN MAKE A SIGNIFICANT DIFFERENCE FOR ETERNITY... YOU CAN DO IT NOW!

Special Announcement

Core Ministries will have a forum section at www.coreministries.com to be used by Pastors, group leaders, and others. Log on to participate in on-line discussions covering many issues, including successful ways others have used the *Wake Up!* Book.

Please send us your best questions for possible insertion in the next reprint of this book.

CONCLUSION

God has given you a candle. Now all you have to do is light it! By the way, He has also given you the matches.

My prayer is that this practical booklet has motivated you to get involved in your ministry! Perhaps it has given you some direction on how to start, and that it guides you through what you can do as you work with others in the Body of Christ. We can all be involved in caregiving.

In her book, *Helping Yourself Help Others*, former first lady Rosalyn Carter, says it much better than I do. She writes, "There are only four kinds of people in this world:

1. Those who have been caregivers.
2. Those who currently are caregivers.
3. Those who will be caregivers.
4. Those who will need caregivers.

That pretty much covers it all."

Let's not trivialize, but if every Christian would light just one tiny candle — what a bright world it would be. I hope I have shown you that God has given you a candle. Now all you have to do is light it! The wonderful thing is, He has also given you the matches.

You are the Giant that needs to wake up. We can become a blazing flame when each of us lights his or her "caregiving" ministry candle. No ministry is too small or unimportant. We do the work and leave the results to Him. The world will be watching us and some may want to become a member of God's family because of the caregiving practices of Christians. (Wouldn't that be wonderful?)

Remember two things about the parable of the Good Samaritan. *Luke 10:25-37* Number one is that Jesus told the story in response to the question, "What must I do to inherit eternal life?" The parable sets forth God's standards of righteousness and shows people that they do not measure up. People need atonement through Christ. The standards are still there to be fulfilled—not for salvation, but out of love for and obedience to Christ — our reasonable response to salvation. *Romans 12:1-2* The second thing to remember is, after Jesus explained how to love your neighbor as yourself, He commanded His audience to . . . "Go and do likewise!"

You have a ministry. If you don't know where to begin, start by making your passion your ministry. Wake the giant in you and start today! The following poem from *The Christian Inmate News* seems to say it well.

Lord Show Us How
By John Bergeson

If we can do some good today,
If we can serve along life's way,
If we have something helpful to say,
Lord, show us how.

If we can right a human wrong,
If we can help to make one strong,
If we can cheer with smile or song
Lord, show us how.

If we can aid one in distress,
If we can make a burden less,
If we can spread more happiness,
Lord, show us how.

Personal Perspective Questions
1. Do you believe God wants you to have a ministry and has given you a specific ministry?
2. It is always nice to have a ministry based upon a Bible verse. What's yours?
3. How has He equipped/prepared you for this specific ministry?
4. Is there anyone else you can talk to who is doing this ministry? Are there any books on it? Have you looked it up on the internet?
5. How will you begin your ministry?
6. In what areas have others failed doing this ministry ? What will be your biggest obstacle to overcome?
7. How much time and money will it take to begin? What other resources do you need?
8. What is the most controversial thing about your ministry idea? What is your biblical defense? (Seek instruction from your pastor if necessary)

Group Discussion Questions

1. Should all *Christians* be involved in at least one ministry? Why or why not?
2. How can we encourage one another to be involved in ministry?
3. How can we teach one another that we "can make a difference"?
4. How do we encourage one another to do it "now"?
5. Should the church take back the responsibility of caring for the needy? If yes — How can this be done? If no — Why not?
6. What is the church's responsibility to the needy? Why should we entrust this work to the world?
7. Is it possible that people can get so busy "doing" they don't have time to "be" with Christ? What advice could we give?

YOU CAN MAKE A SIGNIFICANT DIFFERENCE FOR ETERNITY... AND YOU CAN DO IT NOW!

EPILOGUE

What writing this book helped me to do.

Core Ministries receives hundreds of short articles, poems, puzzles, Bible studies, artwork, and even jokes from inmates. The ones that are printed in *The Christian Inmate News* can strengthen over 200,000 inmate readers (108,000 are mailed and read by more than one inmate). These writings also strengthen the authors as it is good therapy and esteem building for them to see their work in print, especially when it points others to Jesus Christ. Also many non-inmate readers tell Core how much the paper blesses them.

Core has volunteer readers that review every submission and recommend the ones that are most appropriate for the general topic of the current issue. Because of space limitations many are not used. I make the final selection and I always find it hard to decide which writings to include in the paper — there are so many good ones.

In the final week of editing this book, Core received the poem *The Hands of Time* by Bobby E. Rogers. It fit so well with what was written in chapter five that it just had to be included in this book. Two days later *The Christian Inmate News* issue 9 arrived from the printer. In it was the poem *Father — Here I Am* By Krysti Cook, another good example of inmate writing. I thought how nice it would be if more inmates had the opportunity to share their work. Then it dawned on me, Core Ministries just got a new ministry!

Core will publish a book of material selected from those submitted by inmates to *The Christian Inmate News*. This will allow more men and women inmates' work to be shared. The book title will be *Collection of Works by Christian Inmates...BOOK ONE*. Then ...BOOK TWO, ...BOOK THREE, ...etc. You see how easy it is to have a ministry idea?

Who would have thought that the inspiration for a new ministry would come while in the process of writing this book! Turn the page for *Father — Here I Am* by Krysti Cook that sparked the idea to start this new ministry. It along with the two other inmate poems used in this book (*The Hands of Time* by Bobby E. Rogers and *Lord Show Us How* by John Bergeson) will be in BOOK ONE. This will give you an idea of the quality of the writings the book will include. The target date for the first book is December 2000.

Father — Here I am
By Krysti Cook

Father, here I am, your child that went astray,
Although I hear you calling, I can't seem to find my way.

Every time I turn from you, I seem to get further away.
I wonder now if you hear me, when I take the time to pray.

I know that you still love me. You know me better than anyone could
Do I have anything left to offer? Can you find anything that's good?

I know that I am tired, that I want to take another road.
Will you reach down here for me and give me your hand to hold?

No one else can help me, there's no where else to turn.
Can you please rescue me and teach me how to learn?

I want to raise my children - the gifts you gave from above.
I want to teach them about you, to show them how to love.

God you know my heart, you know each thing I feel.
I don't have to pretend because only you know if I am real.

Don't let the devil have me, I am not out of your range.
Just accept me as I am and with your guidance I can change.

Additional Poems Submitted by Inmates for *The Christian Inmate News*

Walk With Me
By Gary Holmes

Walk with me when times are hard
    and troubles are in my way.
Touch me Lord and give me strength
    to make it through the day.
Walk with me when I'm down and feeling
    oh so blue.
Walk with me when I am sick, with a cold,
    fever or flu.
Take my sickness upon Yourself as
    I go in prayer to You.
Walk with me to pass Your Word
    to those who do not know.
Fill me with the Holy Spirit as I move
    from door to door.
Walk with me as I go on to live a better life,
Give me love to carry with me,
    and an angel by my side.
Walk with me, Walk with me, is all
    I ask in prayer.
It gives my heart so much joy to know
    that You are there.

Our Maker and Our Friend
By Bryon Howell

We can do anything with the Lord
We're always heard and never ignored
The Holy Spirit will light our way
Through the darkest night and the
    grayest day

He is Our Maker – He is Our Friend
His Holy Kingdom knows no end
A forgiving God of love and might
Teaching His children how to live right

Even when we are sad and unsure
He gives us the strength we need to
    endure
He is Our Father – loving and true
Praise and worship Him in all that you do.

Discover Your Gifts

Spiritual Gifts

There are many gifts that God has given His people. *Romans 12:6-8; 1 Corinthians 12:27-28; Ephesians 4:11-12* They have been given to us for our common good. *1 Corinthians 12:7* You see, we are all part of one body—toe or eye or ear, weak or strong, honorable or unpresentable. *1 Corinthians 12:12-26* We don't function well without each other. All of us are needed. Each one of us, including you, has been given at least one spiritual gift from God *1 Corinthians 7:7* that is to be used in Kingdom work.

CRC Publications has identified 15 working gifts that are to be used to strengthen and enlarge the Kingdom. CRC has given us permission to reproduce their "Discover Your Gifts" questionnaire. We thank them for the opportunity to help you discover your gift(s). This is a copyrighted document. You should not copy it. If you need more, phone CRC Publications at 1-800-333-8300.

Take the next 20 minutes to start the exciting journey to finding out your gifts.

How To Use This Gifts Analysis Questionnaire

Each statement in the following questionnaire has five response spaces following it:

Very Little – ☐1   Little – ☐2   Some – ☐3   Much – ☐4   Very Much – ☐5

These represent percentages on a scale of 1-100%, as follows:

1. Very little = 0 - 20%
2. Little = 20 - 40%
3. Some = 40 - 60%
4. Much = 60 - 80%
5. Very much = 80 -100%

Read each statement. Decide to what extent the statement is true of you today. Check the appropriate column. (see example below) Your first impressions are usually correct. There are no wrong answers.

Example: I felt that question #20 was true of me some of the time, so I checked box 3.

---

20. I would like to be able to share the gospel freely and effectively with unbelieving persons.   ☐1 ☐2 ☒3 ☐4 ☐5

If most of your checks are placed toward the right or toward the left, don't worry about that. Each person has his own style with questionnaires.

The questionnaire will help you discover your gifts. The results of this questionnaire will be only tentative, however.

THE FOLLOWING IS TRUE OF ME

Very Little – [1] Little – [2] Some – [3] Much – [4] Very Much – [5]

	Very Little	Little	Some	Much	Very Much
1. I am able to organize ideas, tasks, people, and time, for Christian service.	1	2	3	4	5
2. I have used a particular creative ability (writing, painting, drama, etc.) to benefit the body of Christ.	1	2	3	4	5
3. I am able to distinguish between spiritual truth and error.	1	2	3	4	5
4. I have been used to encourage people to live Christ-like lives.	1	2	3	4	5
5. I like to talk about Jesus to those who don't know him.	1	2	3	4	5
6. I have had the experience of knowing God's will with certainty in a specific situation even when concrete evidence was missing.	1	2	3	4	5
7. I assume responsibility for meeting financial needs in church and community.	1	2	3	4	5
8. I enjoy providing a haven for guests and do not feel put upon by unexpected visitors.	1	2	3	4	5
9. I take prayer requests of others seriously and continue to pray for them.	1	2	3	4	5
10. I motivate groups toward specific biblical objectives.	1	2	3	4	5
11. I have a knack for turning compassion into cheerful deeds of kindness.	1	2	3	4	5
12. I have pleaded the cause of God to the people of the church and/or world.	1	2	3	4	5
13. I enjoy doing tasks that help others minister effectively.	1	2	3	4	5
14. I have been responsible for the spiritual lives of Christians with good results.	1	2	3	4	5
15. Content "comes alive" for students (children or adults) when I teach.	1	2	3	4	5
16. I like to plan things in which people are involved.	1	2	3	4	5
17. I would enjoy expressing myself creatively for God through artistic expression (music, drama, poetry, etc.).	1	2	3	4	5
18. I see a serious danger when false teachings and false practices creep into the church.	1	2	3	4	5
19. I am sensitive to suffering, troubled, and discouraged people and want to help them see God's answers to life's problems.	1	2	3	4	5
20. I would like to be able to share the gospel freely and effectively with unbelieving persons.	1	2	3	4	5
21. I find myself accepting God's promises at face value and applying them to given situations without doubt.	1	2	3	4	5
22. I feel moved to give when confronted with financial needs in God's kingdom.	1	2	3	4	5
23. I am sensitive to the acts of kindness which make such a difference for guests or strangers.	1	2	3	4	5

THE FOLLOWING IS TRUE OF ME

Very Little — 1   Little — 2   Some — 3   Much — 4   Very Much — 5

#	Statement	Very Little	Little	Some	Much	Very Much
24.	I am sensitive to the prayer needs of others and concerned to give the needed prayer support.	1	2	3	4	5
25.	I have a desire to help, lead, guide, and direct people in an important church ministry.	1	2	3	4	5
26.	I would like to minister to those who have physical or mental problems.	1	2	3	4	5
27.	I have spiritual insights from the Scriptures relating to people and issues which make me want to speak out.	1	2	3	4	5
28.	I sense when others need a helping hand and am ready to give it.	1	2	3	4	5
29.	I am concerned to see the spiritual needs of believers met and am willing to be personally involved in nurturing and discipling ministries.	1	2	3	4	5
30.	I like to help people understand things.	1	2	3	4	5
31.	I am able to make effective plans to accomplish goals.	1	2	3	4	5
32.	I have significant artistic ability (music, drama, writing, painting, sculpting, etc.) which I have put to good use in God's kingdom.	1	2	3	4	5
33.	I have detected phony or manipulative persons and teachings when others have not.	1	2	3	4	5
34.	People in the Christian community have been stirred up to love and good works by my counsel and encouragement.	1	2	3	4	5
35.	I have been instrumental in leading others to believe in Christ as their Savior.	1	2	3	4	5
36.	In specific cases God has given me assurance that He would do what seemed unlikely.	1	2	3	4	5
37.	I give cheerfully and liberally in support of the Lord's work.	1	2	3	4	5
38.	I have a knack for making strangers feel at ease in my home and at church.	1	2	3	4	5
39.	I pray for others, recognizing that their effectiveness depends upon it.	1	2	3	4	5
40.	I enjoy leading and directing others toward goals and caring for them for the sake of Christ.	1	2	3	4	5
41.	I enjoy working with people who suffer physical, mental or emotional problems.	1	2	3	4	5
42.	I have proclaimed timely and urgent messages from God's Word.	1	2	3	4	5
43.	I like to work at little things that help build the body of Christ.	1	2	3	4	5
44.	I assume responsibility when I see a Christian being led astray.	1	2	3	4	5
45.	I am able to clarify things for learners (children or adults).	1	2	3	4	5
46.	I would enjoy giving oversight to an important church ministry.	1	2	3	4	5

44

THE FOLLOWING IS TRUE OF ME

Very Little – 1   Little – 2   Some – 3   Much – 4   Very Much – 5

	Very Little	Little	Some	Much	Very Much
47. I have the potential to be very creative in an area that could be used in building up the church.	1	2	3	4	5
48. I tend to look beneath the surface and perceive people's motives.	1	2	3	4	5
49. I believe that people will grow to spiritual maturity through counsel and instruction from the Word.	1	2	3	4	5
50. I have a burden for friends and acquaintances who do not believe in Christ.	1	2	3	4	5
51. I have a sense for moments when the "prayer of faith" is needed.	1	2	3	4	5
52. I am willing to maintain a lower standard of living in order to benefit God's work with my financial support.	1	2	3	4	5
53. I tend to be more aware of the needs of guests than of my own.	1	2	3	4	5
54. I have an inner conviction that God works in response to prayer, and I want to be used to help others through prayer.	1	2	3	4	5
55. If I had the opportunity, I would enjoy leading, directing, and motivating others in some aspect of the Lord's work.	1	2	3	4	5
56. The sight of misery makes me want to find a way to express God's love to hurting persons.	1	2	3	4	5
57. Given the opportunity, I would like to be an expository preacher of God's Word.	1	2	3	4	5
58. It is my nature to like to do work that helps others do theirs.	1	2	3	4	5
59. I sense in myself a shepherd's instinct when I know of Christians who need spiritual counsel.	1	2	3	4	5
60. I quickly sense when people (children or adults) are unclear in their thinking.	1	2	3	4	5
61. I have a sense for delegating important tasks to the right people at the right time.	1	2	3	4	5
62. I am aware that people have been blessed through my creative or artistic ability.	1	2	3	4	5
63. I have developed an ability to discriminate between good and evil in today's world.	1	2	3	4	5
64. I am glad when people who need comfort, consolation, encouragement, and counsel seek my help.	1	2	3	4	5
65. I am able to share the gospel in a way that makes it clear and meaningful to nonbelievers.	1	2	3	4	5
66. I am able to go on believing God will act in a situation in spite of evidence to the contrary.	1	2	3	4	5
67. I help people and the Lord's work through generous and timely contributions.	1	2	3	4	5
68. My home is available to those in need of hospitality.	1	2	3	4	5
69. I am conscious of ministering to others as I pray for them.	1	2	3	4	5

THE FOLLOWING IS TRUE OF ME

Very Little – [1] Little – [2] Some – [3] Much – [4] Very Much – [5]

	Very Little	Little	Some	Much	Very Much
70. I have accepted leadership responsibilities and have succeeded in helping a group work toward a goal.	1	2	3	4	5
71. Sick, helpless, and shut-in persons are helped when I minister to them.	1	2	3	4	5
72. God uses me to build up, encourage, and comfort other Christians by speaking to them of spiritual things.	1	2	3	4	5
73. I find practical ways of helping others and gain satisfaction from doing this.	1	2	3	4	5
74. The Lord has used me to watch over, guide, and nurture other believers toward spiritual maturity.	1	2	3	4	5
75. I hold the interest of those I teach.	1	2	3	4	5
76. I have a sense for how and when projects or ministries need to be better organized.	1	2	3	4	5
77. I sense a latent creative ability (in drawing, writing, music, etc.) which I would like to use for the kingdom of God.	1	2	3	4	5
78. I am usually aware of people who pretend to be what they are not.	1	2	3	4	5
79. I would be willing to spend some time each week in a counseling ministry.	1	2	3	4	5
80. I am able to sense when a person doesn't know Jesus Christ, and I hurt for him or her.	1	2	3	4	5
81. I inwardly sense what Jesus meant when he said mountains could be moved by faith.	1	2	3	4	5
82. I have a conviction that all I have belongs to God, and I want to be a good steward.	1	2	3	4	5
83. I have a genuine appreciation for each guest to whom I minister.	1	2	3	4	5
84. I would be pleased if asked to be a prayer partner to someone involved in a ministry.	1	2	3	4	5
85. I am usually quick to sense when a group I am a part of is "spinning its wheels," and I want to do something about it.	1	2	3	4	5
86. I sense when people are hurting in some way.	1	2	3	4	5
87. I think more Christians should speak out on the moral issues of the day, such as abortion, easy sex, racism, and so on.	1	2	3	4	5
88. I wish I had more opportunity to assist others in their ministries.	1	2	3	4	5
89. I would love to be in a position to equip saints for the work of ministry.	1	2	3	4	5
90. I get excited about discovering new ideas I can share with others.	1	2	3	4	5

Now that you have answered the 90 questions, you will want to fill out your "Key Chart" on page 47. Be sure to read the instructions carefully. I filled out the sample on the next page as an example to help you. If you have any questions, ask your pastor for help.

How to Use the Key Chart

Complete the Key Chart on your own. Begin by reading the instructions carefully. (See sample.)

1. Place the numerical value (1-5) for each statement of the questionnaire (1-90) next to the corresponding number in the Key Chart.

2. In Chart A, add each row of three numbers, and write the total in the adjoining box in the "totals A" column. Do the same in "totals B" column for Chart B, adding to the left.

3. Circle the highest scores in the "totals A" column. Circle three or four, but not more than five. Write the names of those gifts in box A, "Working Gifts," with the highest-scored gift first, the next highest second. (In case of ties, it doesn't matter which one is listed first.)

4. Now in the "totals B" column circle the high scores which were not circled in step 3. Write these gifts in box B, "Waiting Gifts," beginning with the highest.

5. Place in box C any gifts not listed in boxes A and B. These are likely not your spiritual gifts, but you have, of course, a responsibility (role) in each of them.

6. Note the gifts in which your "totals B" score is significantly (two or more) higher than your "totals A" score. This may indicate a gift you should develop and use.

Chart A				Totals A	Totals B	Chart B		
1: 5	31: 5	61: 4	Administration	(14)	10	16: 4	46: 2	76: 4
2: 5	32: 5	62: 4	Creative Ability	(14)	8	17: 2	47: 3	77: 3
3: 4	33: 4	63: 4	Discernment	12	(13)	18: 5	48: 4	78: 4
4: 4	34: 4	64: 4	Encouragement	12	(13)	19: 5	49: 5	79: 3
5: 3	35: 3	65: 5	Evangelism	11	9	20: 3	50: 3	80: 3
6: 5	36: 4	66: 4	Faith	(13)	8	21: 4	51: 2	81: 2
7: 5	37: 4	67: 4	Giving	(13)	12	22: 4	52: 3	82: 5
8: 1	38: 3	68: 2	Hospitality	6	9	23: 3	53: 3	83: 3
9: 3	39: 3	69: 3	Intercession	9	9	24: 3	54: 3	84: 3
10: 4	40: 3	70: 5	Leadership	12	(13)	25: 4	55: 5	85: 4
11: 3	41: 2	71: 1	Mercy	6	11	26: 3	56: 4	86: 4
12: 3	42: 4	72: 4	Prophecy	11	11	27: 4	57: 3	87: 4
13: 4	43: 3	73: 5	Service	12	11	28: 4	58: 4	88: 3
14: 3	44: 4	74: 4	Shepherding	11	9	29: 3	59: 3	89: 3
15: 3	45: 4	75: 5	Teaching	12	(14)	30: 5	60: 4	90: 5

BOX A — Working gifts

Highest scored gift	Creative Ability
2nd	Administration
3rd	Faith
4th	Giving
5th	

BOX B — Waiting gifts

Highest not in Box A	Teaching
2nd	Leadership
3rd	Encouragement
4th	Discernment
5th	

BOX C — Not a gift but a role (responsibility)

Evangelism	Mercy	Shepherding
Hospitality	Prophecy	
Intercession	Service	

How to Use the Key Chart

Complete the Key Chart on your own. Begin by reading the instructions carefully. (See sample on preceding page.)

1. Place the numerical value (1-5) for each statement of the questionnaire (1-90) next to the corresponding number in the Key Chart.

2. In Chart A, add each row of three numbers, and write the total in the adjoining box in the "totals A" column. Do the same in "totals B" column for Chart B, adding to the left.

3. Circle the highest scores in the "totals A" column. Circle three or four, but not more than five. Write the names of those gifts in box A, "Working Gifts," with the highest-scored gift first, the next highest second. (In case of ties, it doesn't matter which one is listed first.)

4. Now in the "totals B" column circle the high scores which were not circled in step 3. Write these gifts in box B, "Waiting Gifts," beginning with the highest.

5. Place in box C any gifts not listed in boxes A and B. These are likely not your spiritual gifts, but you have, of course, a responsibility (role) in each of them.

6. Note the gifts in which your "totals B" score is significantly (two or more) higher than your "totals A" score. This may indicate a gift you should develop and use.

Chart A			Totals A	Totals B	Chart B		
1	31	61	Administration		16	46	76
2	32	62	Creative Ability		17	47	77
3	33	63	Discernment		18	48	78
4	34	64	Encouragement		19	49	79
5	35	65	Evangelism		20	50	80
6	36	66	Faith		21	51	81
7	37	67	Giving		22	52	82
8	38	68	Hospitality		23	53	83
9	39	69	Intercession		24	54	84
10	40	70	Leadership		25	55	85
11	41	71	Mercy		26	56	86
12	42	72	Prophecy		27	57	87
13	43	73	Service		28	58	88
14	44	74	Shepherding		29	59	89
15	45	75	Teaching		30	60	90

BOX A — Working gifts

Highest scored
gift_____
2nd_____
3rd_____
4th_____
5th_____

BOX B — Waiting gifts

Highest not in
Box A _____
2nd_____
3rd_____
4th_____
5th_____

BOX C — Not a gift but a role (responsibility)

_____
_____
_____

Once you have finished the Key Chart, continue by reading the following questions and answers.

1. Do I actually have the spiritual gifts I have identified?

Some people are surprised by the gifts which their questionnaire reveals; others are not. Whichever category you fall into, two things must be said. First, congratulations! To be aware of gifts which the Holy Spirit gives is an exciting experience, and very significant. Second, be cautious. You may not actually have the spiritual gifts you identify by taking this questionnaire. Or you may have other gifts not identified here. Two more things should happen before you will be sure what your gifts really are:

a) Others should observe your gifts and tell you what you do well.

b) You should actually use your gifts in ministries and experience a degree of success.

2. What is the difference between a working gift and a waiting gift?

A working gift is a gift you are already using in some way. You may not have recognized it as a spiritual gift, but you were using it nonetheless. You were able to identify working gifts by answering questions aimed at your activities in the kingdom. A waiting gift, on the other hand, is a gift which remains to a large extent undeveloped. There may be hints of it in your activities, but for the most part you haven't used it. However, you do have potential in this area. You cannot identify such a gift simply by looking at activities. Instead you must look at interests, inclinations, sensitivities, attitudes, and concerns. These often reveal a gift waiting to be developed.

3. What am I to do in those areas where I don't have gifts?

Don't think less of yourself because of those gifts which appear in box C, which for you are not gifts but roles. Remember that others have been given gifts in these areas for your sake. Thank God for these gifts and those who have them. In addition, you should encourage and pray for those who have these gifts: they are important to God and his cause. They need the support which you, with your gifts, can give them. Finally, you have a responsibility to be diligent in each of these areas as a member of the church. For example, if evangelism is last on your list, you should recognize that while God may not expect you to be involved in door-to-door visitation, you still have a responsibility to witness.

My friend,
Now that you've got a good
indication of some of your gifts,
use them in the Kingdom for the
glory of God ...1 Timothy 4:14
Dave Ray

Volunteer Hero — Dick Mailman

When I finished the *Inside Brother's Check-Up*, I sent a copy to my mother's pastor in Florida. He gave it to a man in his church who was a volunteer visitor to the Seminole County Jail. His name is Dick Mailman and his story will encourage you. He is one of my volunteer heroes.

The day the pastor gave the book was the day Dick received his reading machine — Dick is blind. Dick stayed up until the middle of the night reading it. He called me the next day and said that it was heaven sent as he had been asked by the county jail chaplain to develop a program to help inmates. Dick had been going to the jail regularly to visit a Sunday school classmate. Dick felt the inmates needed to know that they could find answers for all aspects of their life in the Bible and through a personal relationship with Jesus.

In 1994, When I found out how high recidivism rates were for Christians I was shocked. I wanted to know why. My relationship with Jesus had helped me stay sober, and my new way of life was so much better than my old way. I started research with inmates and ex-offenders and discovered what I felt were the reasons for Christians backsliding to crime upon release. Then I wrote a book to help inmates better serve their time and to prepare them so that when they get out they will stay out.

There is much evidence that involvement by a compassionate volunteer results in a reduction of recidivism by as much as 90 %. Judge Keith Leenhouts started a program of alternate sentencing in 1958, known as VIP, which includes a compassionate volunteer assigned to the convicted criminal. His program has resulted in keeping over two million people from going to jail and prison. The recidivism rate for his program is 7% while the normal rate is 70%. Wow! Therefore, I believe that a compassionate volunteer will have a great effect in the process of rehabilitation. It's important to know that Jesus loves you and forgives your sins but it is very helpful to know that at least one other human being also loves you and accepts you where you are.

Dick Mailman has compassion. Armed with my book and the power of the Holy Spirit he has shown hundreds how they can live a life for Jesus while incarcerated, and that they can prepare for release by applying God's principals from the Bible.

Dick holds 14 classes a week in two jails and one prison in Central Florida. Approximately 400 attend his classes each week. He knows that the recidivism of his students is much less than the norm. Dick does not get paid for what he does. His church buys the materials he uses and they provide the drivers he needs to get to the classes. This is a wonderful partnership between a church and a volunteer to "go into the prisons" as the Bible commands. Although Dick's financial reward is zero his heavenly reward will be great — he wouldn't have it any other way.

Dick and I both know that it is a mystery as to why some go back to crime and others appropriate the born anew experience and live a law-abiding life guided by Jesus. However, from a human standpoint, we know that there are some ingredients that are an important part of the equation.

· Bible study to find practical application to everyday problems (that's where Core Ministries materials can help)
· Participating in discussion with other Christians while incarcerated (*The Christian Inmate News* helps here)
· True forgiveness of oneself and others
· A caring volunteer visitor (That's Dick and thousands of others nationwide)
· A caring church to go to when released
· The inmate's personal commitment to living a life without crime

Dick has made his commitment to serve God in this way and I am so glad. The inmates that experience his classes are truly blessed. I guess that Dick is one of the smartest men I know in applying God's Word and he sees things better than most. I pray that many more come forward and see how spiritually satisfying this type of ministry can be. Dick says that he isn't sure who has learned more, him or the inside brothers.

The key to an effective volunteer is compassion. Core materials will give the compassionate volunteer the confidence to embark on such a ministry. It is not for everyone though it can be just right for others. If you know someone who has compassion and wants to explore this type of volunteerism, have him or her read Core Ministries' *Outside Brother's Check-Up*. They can review our material on the Internet at www.coreministries.com.

I want to encourage compassionate people to explore this type of much needed ministry. Unfortunately most who want to help feel inadequately prepared to do so. Core Ministries resources will help give them the confidence to take a chance for Jesus.

My last request is that you always pray for your volunteers, as Satan does not want them coming in with the gospel.

Your Outside Brother,

Dave Ray

Article taken from a recent issue of *The Christian Inmate News*.

YOUR MINISTRY... anything you do to strengthen others!

HOW TO HELP SOMEONE COME TO KNOW CHRIST
A practical guide for using the *God's Original Plan* booklet for witnessing

Why We Witness?
1. People are lost without Christ. *John 3:36*
2. Witnessing is a God-ordained way to spread His Gospel. *Matthew 28:19*
3. The Lord commands us to witness. *John 15:16; Matthew 28:19*
4. The Love of Christ compels us. *2 Corinthians 5:14*
5. Because you may be the one that God has ordained to carry the message to a particular person.

God's Original Plan **booklet** is not the only way to witness for Christ. It is simply a tool that may make you more effective. It must be remembered that it is the Holy Spirit that convicts of sin and draws people to Himself. He uses many means to accomplish this task, including this booklet. How it works:
1. Clearly, simply and visually presents God's plan of salvation (no language barrier).
2. Gives you confidence because you know what to say and how to say it.
3. Enables you to be brief and stay on track.
4. Enables you to be prepared.
5. Starts on the positive premise that God wants to have a relationship with you.
6. Brings a person to the point of commitment and beyond.

Preparation to Witness
1. Prepare yourself spiritually. Confess your sins and surrender yourself to Christ. *1 John 1:9; Ephesians 5:18*
2. Pray for God's witnessing-opportunity with a person whose heart He has prepared.
3. Pray for God's love to be seen in and through you.
4. Be sensitive to the listener and the leading of the Holy Spirit.

The Simplified Presentation of *God's Original Plan*
1. "Let me tell you how *God's original plan* worked in my life." Tell your own story using just the pictures on the front of the booklet. This is truly sharing your faith and all that it means to you. That is sometimes enough.
2. Then guide the person through the steps for him/ herself.
3. If the person prays to receive Christ, encourage him/her to get a Bible and review the Bible verses on the inside of the booklet.
4. Then go to "What's Next?" near the end of this document.

The Fuller Presentation inside the Booklet
A. The First Four Steps
1. Read or have the person read the question and answer of Step One from the inside of *God's Original Plan* booklet. Hold the booklet so that it can be clearly seen.
2. Read or have the person read the statements that follow the answer. Read the Bible passages that are referenced for each statement. Together look at the pictorial message in the illustration. When finished with Step One, go to Steps Two, Three and Four.
3. Ask for and answer related questions. Offer to answer unrelated questions at the completion the eight steps of *God's Original Plan*.
4. If the person seems unresponsive, ask if the presentation is making sense.
5. If a person is not interested in receiving Christ at this time, give the person the booklet and offer to meet again if that is practical. Make sure that the person understands how to be saved.

B. Encouraging a Person to Receive Christ - Steps Five and Six
1. Explain how Christ may be received through a prayer of repentance, asking for forgiveness and asking Christ to come into your life.
2. Be sensitive. If the person is interested in receiving Christ, pray privately.
3. Go over the prayer for salvation and ask if the prayer expresses the desire of the person's heart. If the person is hesitant to pray, offer to have him or her repeat the prayer after you. You may also say a prayer for the new believer following the prayer for salvation.

C. Assuring The New Believer That Christ is in His or Her Life - Steps Seven and Eight
1. Explain to the new believer that he/she is a Child of God; forgiven and saved forever.
2. Also explain that the new believer now has a relationship with God and can talk to and fellowship with Him.
3. Be sure to explain that salvation is not based on feelings but on the promises of God in the Bible.

What's Next?
1. Go over the next steps on the back page with the new believer. Have him/her fill out and sign the statement at the bottom of the page. Witness it and give the person the booklet. It is their "new birth" certificate. It would be nice if you sent them a card each year on this day.
2. Encourage the new believer to come to church with you or if that is not practical, attend an active local church and become friends with other believers.
3. Disciple the new believer. If you cannot, find someone who will.
4. Assure the new believer of your prayers as he or she progresses in the faith journey. Check up on them periodically.

Extra copies of *God's Original Plan* are available from Core Ministries for $19.95 plus S & H for a pack of 50.

STEP ONE

Question: How can I have a relationship with God?

Answer: I must believe that God loves me and created me to have a personal relationship with Him. The Bible tells me:

- He created me. *Psalm 139:13-14*
- He loves me. *John 3:16*
- He wants me to know Him. *John 17:3*
- He wants me to have an abundant life. *John 10:10*

STEP TWO

Question: If that is the case, then why don't many people have a personal relationship with God?

Answer: Because sin separates man from God. The Bible tells me:

- All of us are sinners. *Romans 3:23*
- When we sin, we are cut off from God. *Isaiah 59:2 Romans 6:23*
- Sin is not doing what we know we should do. *James 4:17*

STEP THREE

Question: How can I fix this separation between God and me?

Answer: Jesus Christ is the only bridge there is between God and Me. The Bible tells me:

- Jesus is the only way. *John 14:6 Acts 4:12*
- He had to die to make the way. *1 Peter 3:18*
- He died for us. *Romans 5:8*
- He proved He was the way by coming back to life. *1 Corinthians 15:3-6*

STEP FOUR

Question: How do I cross this bridge?

Answer: I must personally trust Jesus Christ as my Lord and Savior. The Bible tells me:

- I must trust Jesus. *Ephesians 2:8-9*
- I must become willing to turn away from my sin and turn to God. *Acts 3:19*
- I must receive Christ through faith. *Ephesians 2:8-9 John 1:12; Revelation 3:20*

STEP FIVE

Question: **How do I receive Jesus?**

Answer: **The Bible tells me I must become willing to:**

- **Turn to God, and away from my old way of living.**
  Acts 3:19 Romans 10:13
- **Ask Christ to come into my life.** *Revelation 3:20*
- **Trust God to forgive my sins.** *Acts 2:38; 1 John 1:9*
- **Be willing to let God direct my life.** *John 15:4-6*
  Galatians 2:20

STEP SIX

Question: **I am willing—now what?**

Answer: **I need to pray:**

Dear God, I know that I am a sinner and separated from You. Thank You for sending Jesus to die for me. Please forgive my sins. I ask that Jesus come into my life to help me change my old habits and to live my life for You. I thank You for giving me eternal life. I pray all these things in the name of Jesus Christ.

Amen.

STEP SEVEN

Question: **What now?**

Answer: **I am now a child of God.** *John 3:1-8*

- **He will never leave me.** *Hebrews 13:5*
- **All my sins are forgiven forever.** *Colossians 2:13-14*
- **I will be with Him forever.** *1 John 5:13*
- **The Holy Spirit Lives in me and helps me.** *Galatians 5:25*
- **I am to continue to grow strong & Vigorous.**
  Colossians 2:6-7

STEP EIGHT

Question: **How secure is this new relationship?**

Answer: **The Bible tells me it is forever!**

- **Nothing can separate me from the love of God.**
  Romans 8:38-39
- **No one can cause me to lose this relationship.**
  Isaiah 43:13; John 10:29
- **There is nowhere I can go to get away from God.** *Psalm 139:1-12*
- **No one will snatch me out of God's hand.** *John 10:29*

Question: Is There Anything Else I Need To Do?

Answer: Begin taking steps to grow as a Christian.

- Get a Bible.

- Begin studying the Bible and spend time each day praying and praising God.** God will begin to direct your life in all things.

    Study: *1 Peter 2:2; 2 Timothy 2:15*

    Prayer: *Philippians 4:6; 1 Thessalonians 5:17-18; James 5:16*

    God's Guidance: *Psalm 32:8; Psalm 119:105; John 16:13*

- As soon as it is practical, seek to be baptized. *Matthew 28:19; Mark 16:16*

- When you fail in your efforts to do what God wants, confess and ask for God's forgiveness. *1 John 1:9* Remember that God will never leave you *Hebrews 13:5* and will help you resist when you are tempted to do wrong. *1 Corinthians 10:13*

** Using *The Liberating Devotional* is one way to grow in your relationship with God. A devotional focus tool that helps Christians develop and maintain a consistent, vital devotional life. *The Liberating Devotional* is like an outline—you fill in the details to suit your needs. It is a road map that helps you stay disciplined in having your devotions. See the following page for more information.

On _____ I asked Jesus to forgive me and save me.
                    DATE
I am now born again.

Signature:_____

Witness & Prayer Partner: _____

HE LIBERATING DEVOTIONAL QUICK START

It takes as little as 20 minutes a day!

Devotions are like a three-legged stool. One leg is Bible Reading, one leg is Meditation and one leg is Prayer. Without one of those legs the spiritual stool is unstable and is not able to give us solid support in reaching up to God. By using *The Liberating Devotional* I have discovered that a meaningful devotional life is possible in as little as 20 minutes a day! I have used it for over 18 years and thousands of others use it daily.

This stool is the primary means by which God chooses to communicate with us and to cause us to grow. Keep in mind, our prayers don't need to be long or wordy to be effective. John Bunyan, in his book, Pilgrim's Progress, wrote, "In prayer it is better to have a heart without words than words without a heart." If we use the Lord's Prayer as a model, we can see that the length of time we pray is not the issue. It only has 66 words and it can be said in a matter of seconds.

Getting started:

We suggest using a published daily study guide such as *Our Daily Bread, The Upper Room, Daily Walk, In Touch, Table Talk*, etc.. The study guide will help you reflect on

what God is saying and will suggest personal applications from the verses read. (There are many study guides available— ask a friend or pastor which one they recommend.)

Pick up your pen and get started:

- Fill out A, B, C, D, & E (See "Instructions" on next page.)
- Read the Bible passages suggested in your daily study guide.
- Fill out F with what you got out of the passage
- Read what the study guide author got out of it (It is sometimes different)
- Go on and fill out the rest of the Liberating Devotional (Filling out points G through T skipping the ones that you want.)

Start the recommended 21 Day Bible Study on page 58 as soon as possible — it explains the Bible texts for each item in *The Liberating Devotional*.

SPECIAL NOTES

- As you write daily in *The Liberating Devotional* it is very important to remember that you do not have to fill out every section every day. Some things just won't apply to you every day, or at all, for that matter.

- *The Liberating Devotional* is a tool developed for your personal use. If there are topics you want to pray about that are not listed, use a section that you are not using—or use the Other Prayer Topics section. If you find this devotional confining or intimidating, you are not using the tool to its best advantage. Modify it to your needs—make it yours, and please, don't feel guilty about not filling out each section. Some days you may fill out every section. Other days, God may be speaking to you about one or two areas only. I consider God speaking to me on one issue a success. I hope you will too.

- Realize that you do not have to write a lot. Use short sentences, single words, or some sort of shorthand that you and God understand, so you don't spend all your time writing. After 18 years of use, it still takes me only 20 minutes a day—a manageable amount of time in my busy schedule.

- If you find your mind drifting during your devotional time, it helps to read out loud the Bible verses you're studying and to pray out loud—even if only in a whisper. Everybody's mind drifts during meditation. It's a good idea to have a notepad next to your *Liberating Devotional*. When your mind does drift, you can make a note and then go on with your devotions. These ideas may be about work, relationships or anything you need to do later in the day. As you are praying, be sure to listen to God's ideas and make notes of these too. They may be your marching orders for the day.

- Because you may write things that you would not want others to read, we recommend that you keep your devotional notebook out of sight. We also strongly suggest the use of code words for some items that could be embarrassing or misunderstood. Remember that prayers are for God only, so don't hesitate to disguise your writing to protect the innocent.

Some days are simply going to slip by without you doing your daily devotional sheets. Just pick it up the next day and go on! There is no guilt for missing a day. That's one thing *The Liberating Devotional* will liberate you from—guilt over your devotional life. I have made 90% of the days in the last 18 years but not 100%. For starters why not shoot for three days a week.

> You can create your own *Liberating Devotional* sheets. Use the sample devotional page as your guide along with a blank sheet of paper for each day that you fill out. (You cannot copy the individual sheets as they are copyrighted.) Or see catalog pages at end of this booklet for many styles to choose from. All styles of *The Liberating Devotional* come with an instruction booklet. Proceeds help jail & prison ministry.

Instructions for The Liberating Devotional

DAY/DATE: Record today's day and date here.

YESTERDAY'S WEATHER: Brief note for possible future reference, if it interests you. A way to see God's glory.

RECAP OF YESTERDAY'S EVENTS: This is the journal section you will use when you may need to look back for clarity. What was yesterday's big news? It is a way of keeping track of what God is doing in your life.

HOW HAVE I RELATED TO: (Spouse-Children-Parents-Friends.) These relationships are key to our feelings of well-being. We should make this our first area of concern. This can be as simple or in-depth as needed. Sometimes just using a number from 1 (poor) to 10 (great) works. As with all sections of the devotional, if there is nothing that applies that day, just leave blank.

BIBLE PASSAGE FOR TODAY'S STUDY: As a part of *The Liberating Devotional* system, We recommend that you use a periodically published daily study guide. There are many good ones available. These study guides are helpful because they focus on a short Bible passage and help you then to apply it to your life.

PRACTICAL APPLICATION: Read the study guide's scripture reference, then read the study guide's application. Write down how you can practically apply the passages to your own life. Sometimes you won't see a practical application for you.

SALVATION FOR WHAT LOST PERSON? Pray daily for an unsaved person or family member.

THANKSGIVING TODAY: Gratitude will change your attitude! Always focus on at least one thing that you are grateful for.

MY BIGGEST BURDEN TODAY: Christ said our burden will be light if we trust in Him. Here is where we ask for His help.

CONFESSION TODAY: This is where we get honest before God—to confess sin, including our difficulty forgiving others. Remember, Jesus' blood is sufficient to cover all confessed sin.

DO I OWE ANYONE AN APOLOGY? As you use the devotional more and more you will have less and less need to put a human's name here. Put God's name here if there is not a human to whom you need to apologize.

EMPLOYMENT: Can people tell you are a Christian by your behavior at work? This is an important area to pray about. Our daily work is where and how we spend the majority of our time; it is where we have many of our relationships; and need to make so many choices which impact our lives and the lives of others. God cares about our work, whatever it may be.

As an Employee: What is keeping me from working as unto the Lord?

As an Employer: Do I treat my employees as I would like to be treated? Do I remember they too are children of God?

SPECIAL LEADER: Leaders need wisdom. God places leaders in authority for our benefit. Pray for them.

OTHER PERSON: Pray for God's special grace for someone else.

ANSWERED PRAYER: It is very important to remind ourselves that He works in our lives every day. Remember the poem *Footprints in the Sand*?

ISSUES AT MY LOCAL CHURCH AND MISSIONS: Pray for your Pastor, Sunday School teacher, church programs & board. Pray for individual missionaries and mission organizations.

OTHER PRAYER TOPICS: This area is for anything else you want to pray about. If you need more space in another section simply put an asterisk (*) there and one here and continue writing. However you use this section, make it yours—and form-fit it to your prayer-life. Use the *Special Request* line for that one special thing you want God's help for each day.

DO FOR GOD TODAY: Here is a chance to do something today for the One who has done so much for you. Try to visualize God smiling as you do this deed of love for Him. It could be something as simple as phoning your mother or sharing your faith with a neighbor.

WHAT PROMISES DO I NEED TO KEEP? God keeps His promises—we should keep ours!

HANDLING HIS MONEY: Just how important is it? Of the 33 years Christ lived on earth only 41 days are touched upon in the Bible. Jesus speaks on money issues on 37 of those days. Also, Christ talked more about the use of money than He did about heaven.

The Liberating Devotional

Day/Date	Yesterday's Weather:

Recap of Yesterday's Events:

How Have I Related To: (Spouse-Children-Parents-Friends.)

Bible Passage For Today's Study:

Salvation For What Lost Person?

Thanksgiving Today:

My Biggest Burden Today:

Confession Today:

Do I Owe Anyone An Apology?

Employment:

Special Leader:

Other Person:

Answered Prayer: (Look at past daily devotionals.)

Issues At My Church and/or Missions:

Other Prayer Topics: (Also use for continuations from other sections.)

Special Request:

Do For God Today:

What Promises Do I Need To Keep?

Handling HIS Money: (Is my debt under control?)

© 1992 CORE MINISTRIES

REMEMBER YOU ONLY NEED FILL OUT THOSE ITEMS YOU FEEL MOVED TO FILL OUT

21 Day Suggested Bible Study

Day 1 – **The Liberating Devotional:**
Joshua 1:8; Psalm 5:3.

Day 2 – **How Have I Related To: (spouse)**
1 Corinthians 7:3; Ephesians 5:22-33;
Colossians 3:19; 1 Peter 3:1-7.

Day 3 – **How Have I Related To: (children)**
Proverbs 22:6; Proverbs 23:13; Ephesians 6:4.

Day 4 – **How Have I Related To: (parents)**
Exodus 20:12; Ephesians 6:1-3; 1 Timothy
5:4b

Day 5 – **How Have I Related To: (friends)**
Proverbs 17:17; Ecclesiastes 4:9-10
Philippians 1:3

Day 6 – **Practical Application:**
Psalm 119:18; Acts 17:11; James 1:22

Day 7 – **Salvation For What Lost Person?**
1 Timothy 2:4; 2 Peter 3:9

Day 8 – **Thanksgiving Today:**
Psalm 103:2; Philippians 4:6; Hebrews 12:28
1 Thessalonians 5:18

Day 9 – **My Biggest Burden Today:**
Psalm 55:22; Matthew 7:11; James 1:2-3
1 Peter 5:7

Day 10 – Confession Today:
Psalm 66:18; Colossians 3:13; 1 John 1:9

Day 11 – Do I Owe Anyone An Apology?
Matthew 5:23-24; Romans 12:18; James 5:16

Day 12 - Employment: (work)
Proverbs 16:3; Matthew 7:12; Colossians 3:23
1 Corinthians 10:31; 2 Corinthians 3:12-15

Day 13 - Employment: (as the employee)
Ephesians 6:5-8; Colossians 3:22-24
1 Peter 2:18-21 **(as the employer)**
Ephesians 6:9; Colossians 4:1-6

Day 14 – Special Leader:
1 Timothy 2:1-2; Hebrews 13:17

Day 15 – Other Person:
Deuteronomy 3:28; 1 Samuel 12:23
Matthew 7:12; 1 Timothy 2:1; James 5:16

Day 16 – Answered Prayer: Luke 11:10; James 4:3

Day 17 – Special Issues At My Church: Mark 9:50; Romans 14:13; 1 Corinthians 1:10; Philippians 4:8
Hebrews 10:25. **Missions:** Matthew 28:19; Ephesians 6:18-20; 1 Timothy 6:17-19

Day 18 – Other Prayer Topics: Matthew 21:22; John 16:23-24

Day 19 – Do For God Today: Matthew 5:16; Romans 12:1-2; Ephesians 6:7; James 2:18

Day 20 – What Promises Do I Need To Keep? Numbers 30:2; Psalm 15:1-5; Proverbs 11:3.

Day 21 – Handling His Money: Deuteronomy 8:17-18; Psalm 24:1, 50:10; Proverbs 23:4, 23:11b; Ecclesiastes 5:10
Malachi 3:8-10; Matthew 6:24; Luke 16:11; 1 Corinthians 16:2; 1 Timothy 5:8,6:10; James 2:15-19; 1 John 3:17
(You May Want To Spend More Than One Day On This Important Area)

The Liberating Devotional

Day/Date Sat 8/28	**Yesterday's Weather:** RAINY

Recap of Yesterday's Events: GOT ANGRY WITH JOE AT WORK, BUT I DIDN'T BLOW UP AT HIM. WATCHED SOME TV LAST NIGHT FOR A WHILE, WHAT A WASTE OF MY TIME. SHOULD OF PLAYED WITH THE KIDS INSTEAD! NEXT TIME I'LL TAKE THE WHOLE FAMILY OUT TO PARK WHILE IT'S STILL WARM OUTSIDE.

How Have I Related To: *(Spouse-Children-Parents-Friends.)* HAVEN'T REALLY TALKED WITH MARY FOR 2 WEEKS NOW. I NEED TO OPEN UP TO HER MORE. GOD HELP ME LET HER KNOW WHAT I'M GOING THROUGH AT WORK.

Bible Passage For Today's Study: PSALM 103: 11-12
I NEED TO UNDERSTAND THAT YOU REALLY HAVE REMOVED MY SIN AS FAR AS THE EAST IS FROM THE WEST—THEY NEVER TOUCH. THAT MEANS YOU DON'T SEE MY SIN ONCE I HAVE CONFESSED IT – IT'S GONE.

Salvation For What Lost Person? JASON. GOD WOULD YOU SAVE AND PROTECT HIM.

Thanksgiving Today: FOR MY FORGIVENESS AND FOR YOUR WORD SO I CAN LEARN

My Biggest Burden Today: MARY'S ANGER AT ME.

Confession Today: I'M HAVING A HARD TIME REALLY LETTING GO OF THE BAD THINGS I'VE DONE. IN THE PAST.

Do I Owe Anyone An Apology? MARY AND JASON— HELP ME DO THIS LORD.

Employment: EASING UP ON JOE WHEN HE MAKES MISTAKES. I DON'T KNOW WHY I GET SO MAD. GOD HELP ME BE MORE UNDERSTANDING WITH NEW GUYS.

Special Leader: —

Other Person: MY BROTHER TONY—HE'S SO ANGRY LORD, HELP HIM.

Answered Prayer: *(Look at past daily devotionals.)* YOU HELPED ME TO GET CLOSER WITH MY SON. WE HAVE A REALLY GOOD RELATIONSHIP NOW.

Issues At My Church and/or Missions: GOD, HELP US FIND A NEW YOUTH PASTOR. AND BLESS OUR NEW MISSIONARIES IN CHINA.

Other Prayer Topics: *(Also use for continuations from other sections.)* I'M COMING TO SEE THAT A LOT OF THIS GUILT THING IS THAT I CAN'T FORGIVE MYSELF. PLEASE HELP ME LET GO OF THIS AND QUIT BEATING MYSELF UP. HELP ME TALK WITH MARY AND ASK FOR FORGIVENESS. THEN HELP ME DEAL WITH THEIR ANSWERS. GOD, I WOULD LIKE IT IF SHE REALLY DID FORGIVE ME. GOD PLEASE MAKE JASON UNDERSTAND HOW IMPORTANT IT IS TO STAY IN SCHOOL. IS THERE SOMETHING I CAN SAY TO TONY, OR DO I JUST STAY AWAY FROM HIM?

Special Request: MOM QUITS SMOKING. I WANT THE KIDS TO HAVE A GRANDMOTHER,

Do For God Today: CALL MARY'S FATHER AND SEE IF WE CAN GO VISIT HIM THIS WEEKEND. IT'S BEEN WAY TOO LONG.

What Promises Do I Need To Keep? TAKE THE KIDS TO THE ZOO!

Handling HIS Money: *(Is my debt under control?)* STOP LOOKING AT NEW BOATS THE ONE I HAVE IS PLENTY FOR WHAT WE DO AND IT'S PAID FOR!

© 1992 CORE MINISTRIES

REMEMBER YOU ONLY NEED FILL OUT THOSE ITEMS YOU FEEL MOVED TO FILL OUT

YOU HAVE A MINISTRY... God gave it to you!

The Liberating Devotional

Day/Date	Yesterday's Weather:

Recap of Yesterday's Events:

How Have I Related To: *(Spouse-Children-Parents-Friends.)*

Bible Passage For Today's Study:

Practical Application:

Salvation For What Lost Person?

Thanksgiving Today:

My Biggest Burden Today:

Confession Today:

Do I Owe Anyone An Apology?

Employment:

Answered Prayer: *(Look at past daily devotionals.)*

Issues At My Church and/or Missions:

Other Prayer Topics: *(Also use for continuations from other sections.)*

Special Request:

Do For God Today:

What Promises Do I Need To Keep?

Handling HIS Money: *(Is my debt under control?)*

REMEMBER YOU ONLY NEED FILL OUT THOSE ITEMS YOU FEEL MOVED TO FILL OUT

You Have A Ministry
Index of Major Issues

YOUR MINISTRY... anything you do to strengthen others!

Introducing Core Ministries' Practical Resources for Christian Growth
A new approach to personal growth designed for today's time-pressured life.

In each book discover a real-life application of the Word. Every *Core Ministries* publication is a *Check-Up*—an effective personal growth tool that provides strategies to help bring about spiritual maturity. There is seasoned wisdom in every one of these books—wisdom that has been hammered by the life-experiences of a good observer. These are well designed tools that help the believer work with God to bring about desired maturity and wholeness. All are written by a layman from a layman's perspective.

COMMON TO ALL OF THESE *Check-Ups*

- practical solutions to real life problems
- God is involved in every step along the way
- covers the essence of an issue, not overwhelming
- much scripture throughout
- reusable workbook format that allows for the tracking of progress
- progress, not perfection is the goal
- progress is measured by comparison to self, not others
- God's love, not guilt, is the motivator for change

- user-friendly, molded to the individual reader
- work on one issue at a time, a manageable growth process
- encourages a manageable, meaningful devotional life
- promotes accountability for own behavior through self-evaluation and prayer
- resource list for further help and insight
- transdenominational
- possible to read in a single evening, yet each topic of concern stands on its own and can be read separately in 10 to 20 minutes

MOM'S CHECK-UP . . . A warm, encouraging, and personal book that provides you with practical and positive ways to apply God's truth to the vital role of motherhood. The *Mom's Check-Up* has special information if you are a single mom or are trying to blend two families. It's not something you read through once and put back on the shelf. It's a book you will come back to time and again. *Authors: Dottie McDowell & Dave Ray*

ISBN #1-57326-019-3 .... $14.95

MAN'S CHECK-UP . . . This book helps you evaluate how you are living out the different roles in your life. It also equips you with the tools to bring about change in the areas you discover are not up to God's standard. This is a workbook, a growth tool, a resource for small group discussion. It is also wonderful tool for mentoring or discipling. The *Man's Check-Up* will help you become more like Christ as you work through the Tracking Section and Action Plan that complete this practical application tool. *Author: Dave Ray*

ISBN #1-57326-015-0 .... $9.95

TEEN'S CLINIC . . . An encyclopedia of the issues teens face. Covers 62 issues in a practical, personal and Biblical way that kids find appealing. Will help you and your teens understand that the Bible is relevant to your lives, every day. Written for Christian teens, 13-18 years old, but parents will also benefit from the wisdom here. A great mentoring tool. *Author: Dave Ray*   ISBN #1-57326-021-5 .... $49.95

JOB SEARCH CHECK-UP . . . A practical "How-To" for the job search process. Includes work sheets and focus tools that help organize your search, plus an inventory that helps you evaluate what jobs you are best suited for. But the *Job Search Check-Up* does more. It walks you through the job search process with God involved all the way. *Author: Dave Ray*

ISBN #1-57326-017-7 .... $10.95

PASTORAL SEARCH CHECK-UP . . . The average church congregation goes through this every four years or so. A practical, step-by-step plan to help you find that "right" pastor for your unique congregation. *Author: Dave Ray*

ISBN #1-57326-025-8 .... $19.95 Including the *Pastor's Check-Up*

ONE HOUR MANAGEMENT CHECK-UP . . . A quick, accurate way to pinpoint problem areas in business. A must for the Christian business person. Covers 25 different areas of management. This is a focus tool written for managers by a CEO of 25 years. It is must reading before you hire a consultant to help you solve your problems, so that you hire the consultant with the expertise in your problem area. *Author: Dave Ray*

ISBN #1-57326-020-7 .... $6.95

PASTOR'S CHECK-UP . . . A valuable and objective tool for self- and ministry-evaluation. Helps to identify areas of imbalance in ministry while providing a mechanism for improvement and growth, material every lay leader should know. You can use this tool year in and year out to identify specific areas of concern in your ministry and with God's help, create a personalized plan that strengthens and equips you to serve. While it is a valuable tool for personal evaluation, it is equally effective as a focus for discussions with other pastors and with local church leadership. *Author: Dave Ray*

ISBN #1-57326-016-9 .... $9.95

HEROES OF THE FAITH . . . The stories of 12 African-American Christians whose lives demonstrate the dynamic nature of our Christian faith and the power of God to change the world through the activities of individuals. This book is excellent for evangelism, edification, and discipling adolescent and young adult males. *Authors: Ed McWalters, Paul Schultz and Dave Ray*

ISBN #1-57326-022-3 .... $5.95